9 STEPS
TO BUILD A LIFE OF
MEANING

9 STEPS
TO BUILD A LIFE OF
MEANING

How to Unlock Your Mind, Happiness, Power, and Your Enemy's Demise

RICK WALKER

PRAISE FOR *9 STEPS*

"Walker weaves together wisdom from ancient philosophy, authenticity from his personal autobiography and a profound sense of reverence from the Christian tradition to reflect upon what it means to become a good man leading a meaningful life. However, this is not a theoretical text. Although informed by relevant theory it is about those practices that organically emerged in his quest to find that pathway of transformation to becoming a good man living a good life in a way that is good for others. I admire both Walker's journey and this wonderful book that shares that journey with others so that they can undertake something similar."

DR. JOHN VERVAEKE
Professor of Buddhist Psychology and Cognitive Science, University of Toronto
Author, Awakening from the Meaning Crisis *and* After Socrates

"A thought-provoking and thoroughly valuable read! Packed with timeless advice drawn from the lessons of historical giants, Christian wisdom and the author's own authentic experiences."

GREG BRENNEMAN
Chairman, CEO, President and/or COO of Quiznos Sub, Burger King, PwC Consulting, and Continental Airlines

"These 9 Steps are a catalyst for self-improvement told in a candid and honest manner."

RUSSELL YBARRA
Founder & CEO, Gringo's Tex Mex

"A very worthwhile and meaningful read! The message is clear. Every step you take or don't take in your life should be considered an important choice point. You are either moving toward or away from where you imagine that you could be. Love the innovative roadmap this book gives not just for outwardly success, but for inward peace!"

TONY BUZBEE
Famed Attorney

"Many young men seek role models today. They are wise to do so. Rick has poured his life and his wisdom into this book. It's structured and studded with bullet points and quotes to be accessible. It is filled with contemporary experience and ancient wisdom. It is by a doer, not a pontificator. People will be blessed by this book.

"If you are a young man seeking meaning, wisdom and to be impactful, this book is for you."

PAUL VANDERKLAY
Podcaster

"A profound, refreshing, and triumphantly hopeful way of thinking."

DR. BEN CARSON
17th Secretary of the Department of Housing and Urban Development

Published by Lumicre, LLC

Copyright © Lumicre Publishing

2025

All rights reserved.

The moral right of the author has been asserted.

Hardcover ISBN: 979-8-9926465-4-2
Paperback ISBN: 979-8-9926465-1-1
Audiobook ISBN: 979-8-9926465-2-8
eBook ISBN: 979-8-9926465-3-5

This book is sold and provided subject to the condition that it shall not, by way of trade or otherwise, be lent, resold, hired out, performed, or otherwise circulated without both the publisher's and author's prior consent in any form binding or cover than that in which it is published and without a similar condition including this condition being imported on the subsequent purchaser and reader.

The scanning, uploading, and distributing of this book via any means without permission of the publisher is illegal and punishable by law. No part of this work may be used or reproduced in any manner whatsoever to train or inform artificial intelligence or to teach any computerized system in any way.

This work was first protected under the title *Hope Threatens*.

WWW.RICKWALKER.COM

Book design by Christopher Parker

For my four loves who shine life around our dinner table:

Shannon,

Emerson, Lily-Kate, and Rosie.

Since love lives here, hope blooms everywhere.

Cover: *Hercules Slaying the Hydra* by Jan Müller. The legendary Greek myth originates from the Twelve Labors of Hercules, where he was tasked with defeating the Lernaean Hydra. This serpent-like creature with multiple heads which would regenerate when severed is here depicted as a chaotic, monstrous entity, coiling around Hercules while lunging toward him. Fighting the hydra symbolizes our slaying evil's persistence, misordered values, and the comfortable path to hell. Hercules' muscular form is exaggerated, emphasizing the strength and heroism of this god-man. This is more than a work of art. It is a promise for you. Read Step 5 (Know Joy Requires Pain) to understand the meaning of the cover and the book.

Courtesy: The Met, New York City.
The Elisha Whittelsey Collection, The Elisha Whittelsey Fund, 1956.

View this art in full color and resolution at RickWalker.com/9steps

CONTENTS

FOREWORD x

INTRODUCTION

The Arbitrage of Masterful Ideas   1
A Single Step   3
Book Structure   4
What I Want For You   7

FRICTION

STEP 1: CHOOSE ONE WORTHY ENEMY.   10

The Set-Up: Miami Nights   11
The GQ Party   14
Context: A Goddess Descended   16
Where Are You Right Now?   17
The Problem: Life's Balance   18
The Lesson: Murder The Evil   19
The Theory: Love Requires Hate   21
Your Next Moves   23

PAIR A: OUR INTERNAL DECLINE AND ASCENT

STEP 2: AIM HIGH. AIMING LOW IS THE ONLY SIN.   30

    The Set-Up: I Walked Away in Defeat   31
    My Storm Clouds   33
    My Run for U.S. Congress   34
    Alexander The Low   35
    The Plot: Alexander's Ascent to Power   36
    The Anti-Lesson: The Winning Lie   37
    The Problem: Truth and Success   38
    My Campaign, My Rules   39
    The Votes are Cast   41
    The After-Party   43
    The Theory: Who Are You Becoming?   44
    The Wisest Mind   45
    Your Next Moves   47

STEP 3: PICK A MASTER OR ONE WILL BE THRUST UPON YOU.   54

    The Set-Up: I Met Rembrandt and Aristotle at The Met   55
    The Problem: Men Need Masters   58
    Paradox: How Alexander The Great Became Jewish   59
    An Undestroyable Kingdom Requires An Undestroyable King   66
    The Lesson: Pick a Master Wisely   67
    Life Strategy: Be Mastered   69
    Your Next Moves   71

PAIR B: OUR EXTERNAL DECLINE AND ASCENT

STEP 4: TRUST REVELATION REQUIRES SACRIFICE. 76

    The Fast: My 7-Day Sacrifice — 77
    The Exam — 78
    I Was Stabbed in the Neck — 81
    The Revelation: The Art of a Miracle — 83
    A Wrapped Moment — 84
    The Set-up: Agamemnon — 85
    Your Past Must Be Sacrificed — 86
    Tainted Sacrifices — 87
    Our Rash Vows — 88
    A Bigger Problem: My Mental Fog — 90
    Something's Gotta Give — 91
    Sacrificing 90% of My Net Worth — 92
    My Identity Lost — 94
    Theory: Required Sacrificial Vow — 96
    Your Next Moves — 97

STEP 5: KNOW JOY REQUIRES PAIN. 102

    The Set-Up: Mature Joy is Art — 103
    The Problem: Our Thinking — 105
    The Prophecy: David's Seascape — 106
    Early Takeaways on Pain — 107
    The Stage: Rembrandt's Seascape — 111
    Interpretation: The Painting — 114
    Theory: Easiness Brings Ugliness — 120
    Life Strategy: Pleasure — 121
    Interpretation: Yellow Sweet Tea — 124
    Your Next Moves — 125

PAIR C: OUR MINDSET

STEP 6: EMBRACE THE UNKNOWN.   132

    The Set-up: Flying Swans & Lying Stats   133
    The Sub-Lesson: Trends Don't Matter   134
    How Do I Build A Life That Matters?   135
    Mindset-Shift: Tchaikovsky & Swans   136
    Interpretation: Swan Lake   137
    Theory: Love Requires Vulnerability   140
    Your Next Moves   141

STEP 7: GIVE AWAY WHAT YOU WANT TO KEEP.   148

    The Set-Up: Competency   149
    The Problem: Relevance and Power   151
    Washington and Carson   151
    Slamming the Tyranny   153
    The Lesson: Command Unveils Character   154
    Inversion: The Competent Give   156
    Safety or Meaning. Never Both.   157
    The Law of C.S. Lewis   159
    Your Next Moves   162

DE-FRICTION

STEP 8: ACT LIKE YOU WILL LIVE FOREVER.   170

The Set-Up: Go Watch a Marathon	171
The Problem: What is a Step?	173
Historical: Einstein's Theories	175
Sub-Lesson: Imagining Space-Time	177
An Analogy of The Sun	179
Defeated by a Story	179
The Greatest Duty of Any Man	180
Todays Make Tomorrows	182
Supposition: The Next Evolution of Men	183
Stepping Into Your Evolution	184
The Thesis: The Imbalance Rebalanced	185
Bent Knees Remake Bent Hearts	186
Theory: Christ's Story as Reflection	187
Your Next Moves	189
A Real Girl's More Than A Fake Father	193

CONCLUSION

STEP 9: SEEK BEAUTY AND YOU MAY FIND TRUTH. 198

    The Set-Up: Selfish College Sex   199
    The Problem: Where To Begin?   203
    What Is The Maximal Love?   204
    Inversion: False Contentment   208
    Sometimes Wandering is Prayer   209
    I Was Blind, But Now I See   210
    My Revelation Became My Evolution   214
    Your Lesson: A Magical Living Canvas   215
    Theory: Rembrandt   215
    Theory: Love & Virtue   218
    My Financial Evolution Begins   218
    Preparing For Your Next Moves   220
    Your Next Moves   222

EPILOGUE

    Alexander in Samaria   233
    Actions for an Asymmetric Life Now   240
    Works Cited   241
    Artworks Cited   241

"There is a set of advantages that have to do with material resources, and there is a set that have to do with the absence of material resources—and the reason underdogs win as often as they do is that the latter is sometimes every bit the equal of the former."

MALCOLM GLADWELL
David and Goliath

FOREWORD

Dan Crenshaw

United States Representative and Navy SEAL
Author, *Fortitude*—a *New York Times* bestseller

IT MIGHT SEEM odd that a former political opponent would write the foreword for this book, and yet here we are. I met Rick for the first time at one of our first candidate forums, hosted by the Houston Pastor's Council. It was our first foray into public life. I was nervous, I assume he was too. Then again, considering his profound breadth of knowledge of Scripture, he was probably a tad less nervous than I.

On another occasion during that primary election for Texas' 2nd Congressional District of the U.S. House, we were both lingering in the parking lot of the Kingwood Community Center, handing flyers to voters before they entered the building to vote. We exchanged jokes, took some pictures. I may have even told some voters that "Rick Walker is more of a cat person than a dog person." That was about the extent of our political attacks against one another. Oh, how times have changed.

Today's world is not one characterized by the cordial competition that I recall with Rick. Instead it is characterized by outrage and attention-seeking, driven fundamentally by a lack of purpose.

When men lack purpose, they resort to ignoble aims.

This realization is what perhaps drove me to write *Fortitude* in 2020, and it is what drives me now to recommend *9 Steps*, which is, fundamentally, a book about discovering purpose and meaning.

As Americans, we have much to live up to. Our republic was founded by a young cohort of geniuses that enabled our generation to live the most prosperous and comfortable life in human history. You might say a bit of gratitude is in order, and yet it's hard to come by these days.

America persists as one of humanity's greatest ideals. The shining city on the hill. A republic founded on the principle that government exists to protect the God-given rights of its citizens. Not just the rights to speak freely, own property, and pursue one's happiness. Those are the obvious ones. We wrote them into our Constitution, in fact. It is also the right to take risks, to fail and then succeed, unburdened by the whims of low-aiming men. Preserving this legacy and the spirit that defines America is no small feat. It demands constant effort, vigilance, and above all—a renewal of personal responsibility. Our republic fails without a dutiful citizenry.

Just as your muscles will atrophy without use, the cultural fabric that underwrote our success will atrophy without persistent vigilance. It is not enough to acknowledge the right ideals, we must also live them, and we must build the habits to make them endure.

To be a good man—and by that I mean a man who leaves the world even slightly better than you found it—you must embrace the challenge of responsibility: live with fortitude, inspire action, and defend those you love. How you do this is up to you.

I have come to know Rick as one of these good men. He loves his country and his family. He has been a loyal friend to me in a world where I am betrayed constantly. He's a straight-shooter. Maybe too straight sometimes (I suppose we have that in common). Leadership is not the art of telling you what you want to hear, but what you need to hear. And make no mistake, what you need to hear is truth. Be wary of the crafty demagogue who mirrors your emotions and opinions for the sake of gaining your favor.

Rick is a leader and a truth-teller. He's a businessman, yes, but also a philosopher and a scholar. You will not find tired old platitudes in his writing, because Rick is someone who has actually bothered to think original thoughts, a rarity in today's literature. In *9 Steps*, he reveals the steps that brought him, and countless others, into a life of purpose.

That's what this book is all about: taking steps toward your purpose.

You must demand more from yourself than others. You must reject the desire to be a victim and adopt the mindset of a victor. Not because you can, but because you must.

In 2012, I was struck by an IED in Afghanistan and left blind for weeks. Doctors doubted I would ever see again. It was one of the hardest physical challenges I've faced. But one thought stuck in my head. I knew others had faced far worse. Many of my teammates had paid far greater prices. My own mother had faced a far greater battle against cancer while raising two obnoxious young boys, and yet I can't recall a single moment of self-pity or resentment from her. Sometimes a bit of perspective can get you through the hard times and onward to the higher aims that your world requires of you.

Perspective allows you to feel gratitude, and from gratitude comes hope. Hope is the main ingredient for perseverance. As a man of fortitude, you do not wallow in despair; you overcome, you persevere.

There are many Americans who feel lost, walking through a meaningless desert, wondering what their purpose might be. It's easy to feel that way in today's digital paradox where we are simultaneously more connected and less connected than ever.

There is no easy answer to building a meaningful life. Like anything worth building, it is built in steps. Perhaps the following pages will help you along some of those first steps.

Enjoy.

DAN CRENSHAW
United States Representative and Navy SEAL

*"Wait for it patiently—
annihilation or
metamorphosis."*
MARCUS AURELIUS

INTRODUCTION

THE ARBITRAGE OF MASTERFUL IDEAS

My Dad and I were both out of work one summer. So we'd visit yard sales to ask if they'd sell us their old gold watches. They'd run inside to find them. We'd purchase, polish, then pitch those timepieces to nearby collectors for a small profit.

Everyone inherits that cigar box of tangled jewelry. They place it up on the bookshelf then forget about it. Sitting in the shadows of dusty wisdom. Men rarely value what they don't earn.

As I turned sixteen, my Mom and Dad bought my first car with some of the profits he earned from his watch sales. A 1988 sun-worn red Chrysler LeBaron. My buddy and I would often head, windows open, out to Padre Island with our surfboards strapped to the roof rails with a detour to the grocery store to buy whatever meat was on sale that day to grill at the beach. And if you know your geography and how close Corpus Christi is to Mexico, you'll understand we weren't having steaks. It was beef tongue, cheek, goat, and the occasional pig feet for us broke teenagers. But we were happy to be on the buying end at the right price, and they were glad to discount it instead of throwing it out expired. Because if you're on the beach with fresh flour tortillas, you will buy, grill, and happily eat almost anything.

And buying a case of hot bottled water and a bag of ice at the store, then selling it for ten times more on the blazing beach, we earned tomorrow's gas money while we ate today's tacos.

My parents paid $600 for that car, and it lasted me until college when with 43,000 more miles, I sold it for double to a guy who needed to get to his fiancé in Tulsa that day. He paid up because his longing for her appreciated into reality once he arrived where his love lived.

My Dad taught me about cars, life, watches, and the business of arbitrage.

Arbitrage occurs when there is a value inefficiency between two owners or two places. We bought low from an unprofessional in an inefficient market, then sold the watches to collectors who knew their true value was not in sitting in forgotten junk boxes up on shelves.

Today, the world's most successful families and institutions trust me to build their wealth by arbitraging various investments. And beyond business, arbitrage has been the steady framework I've used to methodically rebuild my personal life when it was stripped away from me.

This book is about the arbitrage of masterful ideas: taking undervalued and overlooked wisdom and using it to build all that is most valuable in life. Unbeatable focus. Unstoppable fortitude. Incredible resilience. True honor. A flourishing family. Influence. And more. Much more. The result is wealth of a kind that no gold can purchase: a life of true and deep meaning.

To get there takes a journey of just 9 Steps. I say "just" but this is no throwaway list of top tips. They travel a narrow path toward that life of meaning—and to walk them is to undergo a profound evolution. I found them through trial and error, and I will share my process of discovery with you.

Wisdom is a deeper and older thing; and we will meet and learn from many souls, both young and old, who have much to teach us along the way.

I've used this arbitrage as a map to transform my life. First to cut away my cobweb-like ego. In that self-education, I cleared away the jungle of my lostness and the expectations heaped on me by others, to tromp forward with what I love most: family, history, stories, strategy, and mentoring others. And suddenly clearing out of the shaded labyrinth the sun's brilliance unveiled the way to meaning. A path glimmering with the wisdom which guided my wandering feet out of the wilderness. And into an adventure you too can experience.

It's a quiet path. Always there. Some have walked it, or claimed to. But the loud vulgarity of our ambition to invent our own meaning has caused most of us to miss it. We've wandered without a map of purpose to guide us. Until now.

These 9 Steps worked for me across various contexts: escaping my hopeless life without resources, founding and growing a business into six states, scaling an international nonprofit into fifty countries, advising the world's elite through tragedy, and polishing up my own life. I tripped up on my way there. But I found a life of true meaning and achievement. You can and will as well.

I'd like to think you and I can relate to each other. Look beyond the specific details of our experiences, lifestyles, and stories. I offer you an authentic perspective into my raw mistakes so you can believe these 9 Steps are possible for you too—no matter what you've done or where you've messed up. Allow me to be your trusted guide—with the map to get you onto this path. A path bricked by great books and masterpieces.

Broken-bound books and cracked canvas frames on forgotten dusty shelves contained the wisdom I missed. Assuming they were worthless, I never realized that they could unlock disproportionate relevance, hope, and wealth in the higher marketplace of my real life if they were just offered a little light with a bit of my attention.

Not by looking in them. But by looking for my revelation through them.

And your revelation begins with a single step.

A SINGLE STEP

But I suspect you have been standing around just like me.
    Fearing.
        Planning.
            Waiting.
Waiting for that risk-free moment. That work-free glory.

That justified excuse we've used to avoid real opportunities which always means the potential of failure.

Actionless and stepless.

Frozen in fear, we both stand here as life ticks by. And the minute we get a taste of success our imposter syndrome kicks in to resurface self-doubt and the horror we'll be discovered as the worst versions of ourselves. And sell ourselves short.

This standing poisons our minds with mediocrity.

"If I can just keep doing this work I hate for another twenty years I can get out of here with a pension. If he would just notice how smart I am, I'd earn what I want to make. If I could just speak up for myself they would stop taking advantage of me. If I could just put her in her place she'd respect me. If I just had a safety net I could take that risk."

I still have those thoughts too—a bit of money and success won't change that.

My friend, the hour to end your standing is here.

Standing only ends with a step. Just one step can push you out of your present to get you closer to your future. Those failures and regrets would be left behind if you had the energy and proven plan to do it. Right?

In life, the steps you take will either get you closer or further from the best possible version of yourself. There are no sideways steps. Your actions each lead to either a life of hellish regret or heavenly redemption.

When you order your steps and put a few together, perhaps you might even begin to create some traction in your life. You'll realize that pains, struggles, wrongs, and frictions are all just opportunities to help you move forward. Traction is only friction which is flipped into an opportunity with more grip.

And when you can put a few of these steps together with some traction and grit, you might even form a stride and move down the pathway toward your destiny. After all, strides are only a collection of steps to chase the higher call ahead of you.

The steps I took resurrected me from the stands I didn't.

BOOK STRUCTURE

This book of 9 Steps is the gift I wish I had. The plan I suspect men need. For men who want to truly live a life instead of faking one.

Every step—in a race or in this book—is both a vertical lift and a horizontal lean forward into the next stride. Let's begin by talking about the horizontal part of the structure: the world you can see. The horizontal component includes the lessons I learned from the failures and successes in my twenties and thirties:

- scaling an international organization from 800 to 2,000 team members as Chairman,
- finding and losing love,
- building a family with the love of my life,
- running for United States Congress,
- building my first company from 0 to 400 employees at 26, and
- undergoing a brain-changing surgery.

Much of it at the same time. Hell, even terrorists wanting me dead.

The Horizontal

I want to show you how I did all that and you can do even more. These 9 Steps revolutionized my mind, heart, and strategy to pull me out of despair, poverty, and mediocrity. They are concrete. You can see and know whether or not you are taking them. They are useful alone, but earth-shattering when taken all together.

These 9 Steps blaze with fresh energy. Empowering your momentum to overtake that next inch of ground and destroying whatever blind spots are in your way. We didn't have to know how the mechanics of those watch components worked, just that they did. And this is wild, I know, but if you will just accept these 9 Steps as promises, somehow, without understanding the mechanism, your true purpose will be magicked into you.

Chapter	The Step
Step 1	Choose one worthy enemy.
Step 2	Aim high. Aiming low is the only sin.
Step 3	Pick a master or one will be thrust upon you.
Step 4	Trust revelation requires sacrifice.
Step 5	Embrace the unknown.
Step 6	Know joy requires pain.
Step 7	Give away what you want to keep.
Step 8	Act like you will live forever.
Step 9	Seek beauty and you may find truth.

So those 9 Steps are the actions comprising the horizontal part of our plan: the world and the self you can observe in front of you.

And if you're like me, when you begin to pick up the pace into a full sprint, you actually fly a bit in those split moments between your grounded steps. But be warned: the 9 Steps above are only the horizontal plane of each action. And though they will dramatically improve your life, you will not get their full dimensionality without their vertical component as well. Sometimes, you will be curious to know why the mechanics work, not just that they indeed do work. So the vertical parts are there to explain that.

The Vertical

The vertical dimension of each step also bounds us upward into a higher calling as well. Each step is paired with another in chapter pairs. Paired as paradoxical contrasts or complete inversions. And here is where our map will give us the higher wisdom found through arbitrage.

Friction: We begin our journey with Step 1—Choose One Worthy Enemy—in the transparency of my heathen pride. I was a half-cultural Christian living with a selfish and fully agnostic bent. And that internal friction between those sides of me were at war. Many of you can relate to me in this tension: work and home, purpose and provision, past and future, risk and reward.

Chapter Pair A: Our Internal Decline and Ascent After the introduction, we will cover a chapter (Step 2) about the internal decline of Alexander the Great, where I will share a little about my moral descent as well. You and I are more like Alexander the Great than we know, so we will see ourselves in him. Then, in chapter 3 (Step 3), Alexander's unexpected moral ascent will provide you with a small glimpse of what is possible as we get our internal lives in order.

Chapter Pair B: Our External Decline and Ascent The second pair, in Steps 4 and 5, concerns our external lives and how reality really works. Here, we will move to evaluate the external descent, the circumstances we can't control and the inversion out of them using two of the most famous seascapes ever. These stories of men like us set in seascapes—one a myth and the other historical—display the struggles all men deal with regardless of experience or wealth. Surfboard or ship.

Chapter Pair C: Our Mindset The third chapter pair—Steps 6 and 7—reorients our thinking by looking at two of the most competent men who have ever lived—President George Washington and Secretary Ben Carson. Their lives—the first of fatherly tyranny and the second of skillful purity—help us discover the treasures hiding within our fear, vulnerability, and competency to defeat the evil problems we see all around us. This is a new vision of thinking for regular guys like you and me.

De-Friction: And we complete the pairing of struggles from Step 1 with the final Step 8. This is where the tensions of my life were resolved. Where the friction at the beginning is seen to be mere grip to launch me off the starting line. We arrive at the proper vertical thinking about the internal and external factors that matter. This is the sometimes embarrassingly obvious yet rare wisdom we really need to escape the gravity of our circumstances no matter how hard we try.

Conclusion: And finally, we will end with my Alexander-like revelation in Step 9 which forced all the other steps toward what I can only call an evolution. And since you and I are so much alike, I suspect you also can get there.

This story-led wisdom glues the horizontal actions to the vertical morality, yielding a powerful leap in your advantage.

I feel an altruistic call to share the story of how I discovered that leap out of my own once-miserable life. I feel it can help you step out of the hellish stickiness you've been trying to escape. I found a truer path, a purpose, that I once assumed was unavailable and that purpose unstuck my life to get me ready to leap up to the next level.

So, this is a calling for me. To you. And my calling comes wrapped in some of the best stories I could find to share with you.

Chapter Structure

These 9 Steps are delivered in 9 self-contained chapters in the same packaged form:

- Historical/Personal Story
- Set-up/The Problem
- Historical/Personal Context
- Facts/Lessons
- Theory
- Your Next Moves

Each chapter concludes with Your Next Moves. These practical actions are based on the personal, historical, philosophical, and theoretical lessons I've used. If you get bogged down in the Theory, always know there's a reset at the end of each chapter.

WHAT I WANT FOR YOU

In this book, I don't want you concerned with making money. Too petty. Or converted to a rigorous religion. Too constraining. Or engaged in toxic masculinity. Too selfish. I want more for you.

I want to rip away the comfort now enslaving your potential. And imagine if one man's want could threaten your longing for ease.

You'll find this book is a hybrid memoir with a self-improvement theme. Because why would I ever write about myself without trying to help others? Why would I ever try to help others without using the lessons I've learned myself? I'm not a boring theoretician after all.

Ask yourself:

- "What would the most optimistic person who's ever deeply loved me wish for me?
- What if one win could wash away all my excuse-filled losses?
- Am I willing to evolve into the kind of man who can one day bear the responsibility of a family? Or, God forbid, an entire company of families?
- Can someone else's hope revolutionize my hopelessness?"

And within those questions, your potential lurks.

In the shadows.

In the murkiness of dusty shelves and the gloom of broken hopes.

Perhaps your vices, virtues, convictions, and proclivities—the ones you've been told were worthless and should bury in a box—could be resurrected as valuable treasures if they were just noticed from the right angle.

Some shelved hopes shimmer only in the sun's polishing rays. Arbitraged like a golden Rolex whose value was always misunderstood by those same novices who once misunderstood you; those misled men who whispered weakness in your ear because they felt threatened to live with passion in their hearts.

You see, my friend, I believe if a drop of hope exists somewhere, it threatens all threats everywhere. And I suspect hope now lurks in the dark with a desire to blaze forth the infinitely valuable possibilities of what you could achieve with a couple of these steps.

> *If a drop of hope exists somewhere,*
> *it threatens all threats everywhere.*

And over the next thirty seconds, you'll discover I may know a little about threats.

FRICTION

"We cannot afford to be naive about evil—it must be faced. But we cannot be intimidated by it either. It will be used by God to bring good. For it is one of the most extraordinary aspects of the good news that God uses bad men to accomplish his good purposes.

"The great paradox of judgment is that evil becomes fuel in the furnace of salvation."

EUGENE H. PETERSON
Run With the Horses

STEP 1

CHOOSE ONE WORTHY ENEMY.

*If you don't know what you want,
never start with a goal.
Start with an enemy.*

THE SET-UP: MIAMI NIGHTS

THE BEHEADING DVD arrived days before I was to attend an invite-only event for future global leaders co-hosted by former U.S. President Bill Clinton's Foundation. It was 2009, and for plausible deniability's sake, let's say I was NOT involved in a nonprofit's PSYOP (psychological operation), which essentially "neutralized" a million enemy combatants.

But we threatened them with something worse than death.

Some of us quietly funded various philosophical, social, and faith efforts in various countries north of the Sahel region of Africa. This region is quite strategic: easy access through Libya into Egypt, across the Sinai Peninsula through Saudi Arabia, and into Iraq and Syria.

The West had been in the throes of its war on terror. Some of us business people wanted to help. I had just turned thirty and raised $20 million over several years to infiltrate media, humanitarian aid, and religious organizations. I eventually became Chairman.

We introduced a variety of concepts that secularized certain key populations. If a dedicated adherent becomes a secular mercenary, his commitment to extremism wanes. He doesn't have to deconvert. It's the true believers who convince their own children to savagely blow themselves up. And that's the part you're not supposed to say.

The enemies of humanity FedEx'd us the day after leadership meetings in Niger and Mali. Playing the enclosed DVD. We saw our local leader wearing an orange jumpsuit. The masked cowards in all-black attempted to deconvert him from his apostasy.

Refusing, our colleague began to be beheaded on video. Not able to fully decapitate him, to saw. Vile creatures of evil hate.

Sweat dripping from my armpits down my sides—wondering if my family was safe—I watched the video in putrid horror as his neck bones ground against those bladed teeth. This was not the first killing. There had been 52 other team members murdered by that time—one for each week of the year. Evil has teeth. And it threatens to kill us all.

And the evils of the world became not only more real, but more proximate for me. Nameless and faceless, except for the smudged fingerprints all over the disc. The whiff of death was close enough to smell their sandy sweat on that envelope and I knew these far-away extremists on

> "The world is a dangerous place to live, not because of the people who are evil, but because of the people who don't do anything about it."
>
> ALBERT EINSTEIN

television now could enter our homes as they could ship bugs, poisons, explosives, or threats without a single person in-country. Terrorize without presence. They knew our names and addresses. The double oceans of American safety no longer protected any of us.

The academic and business books written by forgettable men tell you to start with a goal. They don't know what they're talking about. Don't tell me about your goals, tell me about your enemies and the problems which break your heart.

Most men need worthy enemies more than they need friends.

That day, however, with evil's threats now closer than ever, I felt an overwhelming desire for a truer good to guide my life. And to stand up to evil. If my shaking legs could.

Choose one worthy enemy.

I was invited to the global leadership event in South Florida because of my business background as a fairly successful young founder and because I was the person back then who did the type of charitable work that deconverted a million terrorists. It was odd that they found out about it since this is the first time I've ever really mentioned it publicly. But I showed up in Miami wrestling with the anxiety of my more exposed situation but also a strong sense of ego as I was being considered a leader of the future. My life felt like it was opening up. But suddenly much more vulnerable.

And my imposter syndrome was in full swing.

With that mindset, I dove into the serious work of the Miami event. We spent the week discussing how to save the planet, running on the beach, setting up b-corps (a hybrid between a business and a nonprofit), and planning how soon we could exit our current businesses at a time when purchases of tech companies were astronomical—often 50-80 times earnings, these exit scenarios were enough to ensure most of these 20-somethings never had to work again. I'd bet most of today's billionaires under forty-five attended.

The evenings began with a three-hour dinner at a rented restaurant—lobsters, Wagyu, and celebrity chefs. Aged wines, bourbons, and Smirnoff flowing. The conversations were amazing: three-day work binges, drug optimization, market hacking, offshore moves, investment buybacks.

They were 300 of the smartest thinkers alive, and I suspect most of them were on at least two of the great leadership drugs of the time: Adderall, cocaine, and Provigil (modafinil). Half proactively told me they were on something. These leadership cocktails, mixed with others including mushrooms, meditation, and alcohol, allowed many to augment their mental state and provided stamina for projects. Or better personalities. Some told me they would get by with only sleeping three times per week during big pushes. I thought about being able to sit and work in an ultra-focused state for twenty-four straight hours. An extended flow-state. I imagined it would be an amazingly competitive advantage—and early death. I didn't have the drive to try.

> *"If death meant just leaving the stage long enough to change costume and come back as a new character ... Would you slow down? Or speed up?"*
>
> CHUCK PALAHNIUK
> (AUTHOR OF *Fight Club*)

Though many of these men could not listen passively, they had to verbally assent to whatever the other person said. "Yeahyeahyeah" fired rapidly, but I was one of the few who had not built a true tech company, and one of the few not from either coast. And certainly not on cocaine. I didn't belong. I was likely five years older and just in a different place in life. For me, I was in the unique position of being impressed by their younger intellects while pitying them as persons.

I was from Texas, after all. All the ultra-successful business people I knew back home were in their fifties and sixties. Normal oil and gas CEOs. Mostly alcoholics with stable personal lives with their prenup'd fifth wives. These wives were not originally as attractive as the first ones, just younger and fitter. But not unsolvable. All these guys had their "standard program" over at the Lind Institute of Plastic Surgery. Money buys happiness. But never joy.

Following the nightly dinner, the hosts rented a nice little homemade gelato shop. For the first trip, we'd pop by for a single scoop of Pistachio on a waffle cone. Since it was available to us anytime between eight at night and three in the morning, that was a twice-per-night event. The second trip was typically a sweet cream option in a waffle cup to mix things up. I called my wife to check in most mornings after breakfast and again at night walking to or from gelato. Our daughter Emerson was one then, and Shannon was back home in Houston, caring for her in the real world.

THE GQ PARTY

Then there were the parties. Beginning around ten-thirty. Smirnoff hosted one night. Mercedes-Benz, another. And a GQ party the final night. And everyone knows—like wines—save the best for last.

I only found one other married guy among all those leaders, so we hung together. We were around thirty, old men for that crowd, and discussed our wives, kids, families, and business. He was a billionaire's son groomed to take over the family's investments: a large publicly traded company and a professional sports team. And so, when we arrived at the GQ party, we grabbed Dr. Peppers with a splash of grenadine and headed out to the back lawn. I didn't drink at all, so my low-energy personality starkly contrasted the high-imagery vibes rumbling throughout the younger crowd.

Somebody told us the party mansion was formerly a Jewish synagogue. It was all white stucco, with Miami palms. The uplights accented the triple-story Mediterranean architectural accents. Multiple bars poured generous drinks throughout. The DJ's techno-jams thumped as things got going. And it was only eleven. It certainly had the Playboyesque vibe. Cigar smoke hung in the air, with a sour twang.

I imagined Solomon, the Jewish king with 300 concubines, would enjoy this. He, David's son, was the king who built the first temple. He spent seven years building that temple but thirteen years building his own house. His palace was even larger than the temple, boasting cedars of Lebanon, precious stones, and the finest artwork. His home was even said to have a Hall of Judgement where he would sit on a throne to hear legal disputes and make declarations in front of large audiences. I had some judgement calls to make myself later. We all do.

If I say the backyard had a pool, it would be an offense to water because the football-field-length modern fountain beamed as every dance step seemed coordinated with the pulsing energy edged by the boxed hedges surrounding the pool for privacy, then met the green palms perfectly lining the deck where twenty-four king-sized beds covered in linens and flowers lay. Beds not for me.

Then arrived the futures of our world. The heroes NASA would come to if the world was in crisis from aliens or asteroids. And they strutted in, pimpled cocks flaunting their misfitted blazers with ripped jeans.

Colored sneakers and flip-flops. Those in Toms had just come from Austin's SXSW Music Festival. Just as Miami Billionaires today rock timeless Concetto Limone loafers to the opera.

Some only had one. Many had two. But, the sleaziest had three "models" on each arm as they strode past us out by the sparkling water splashed by fountains. Twenty-year-old rebels of knowledge with thirty-year-old models of savvy. The knock-off Chanel No. 5, with a hint of Marlboro, tainted our air as they passed. A warm summer night about to grow hotter. South Beach style. These women were all over. Brunettes and fake blondes. And more showed up without dates but needed one. I may just have still been on edge about the DVD. I was incredibly paranoid. I wasn't just a married man, I was a happily married man. I felt like I was getting a glimpse at how South Beach's cocaine trade had fueled a generation of false truths and fake loves.

But as I heard later through the grapevine, modeling wasn't their only gig:

Many of these tech executives had access not only to wealth but data. Data on people and companies, their secrets, their desires. And though they suspected women wanted them for their money, their access to data was perhaps most attractable to a certain sort.

The next morning at breakfast, as the guys began dragging back in, or coming down from their rooms, I heard the theme was the same.

"Did you ever leave your phone last night?"

I heard one awoke to find a device plugged into his phone which his new friend quickly unplugged then made an excuse to leave. Another uncharacteristically left his phone in the bedroom to take a shower and didn't know why his guest was gone when he returned. They pulled their SIMs and storage cards, tossed their batteries, and wrapped their Blackberries in aluminum foil as a make-shift Faraday cage until they got back home to investigate. "NoNoNo!!"

If the suspicions were right, some of the smartest men in the world were perhaps duped by Russian agents.

I was relieved when I heard about it. Relieved I left. Sometimes where I am NOT is more important than where I am. That party didn't feel right to me. It felt more like a Five Guys fries and an extra scoop of sweet cream gelato kind of night for me. I wasn't interested in them throwing a velvet bag over my head and scooping me into a black van. I had seen what others wished to do with my head in a bag, and I wasn't even certain I could tell the difference between Russian and Persian talent. I couldn't even handle my smoke-show wife back home.

*Sometimes where I am NOT
is more important than where I am.*
_____

WHERE I wanted to be, told me more about WHO I could be. I gladly headed home the next day, without the layover in Siberia or Syria. With my phone. I knew I should avoid temptations like these because they have no upside benefit to counter the downside risk.

DVD-sending beheaders must themselves be beheaded. And they told me a hundred of our brave men descended on where those masked evil men murdered our one good man. Because you don't send one bullet when you can send a hundred. A hundred wasn't needed, but it was what was right.

As a man of shaky but deep faith, I believe lavishness is always right when dealing with evil—and with love.

Don't send a single rose when you can send a hundred.

Imagine your life as a wise adventurer. Imagine your future self, full of discipline and vigor, and ask yourself,

- "How can I practice lavish courage?
- What foolish activities only bring me catastrophic risk, without any potential upside?
- What is possible with a hopeless life like mine?
- Can a man like me be loved by a woman like her?
- Am I being called to launch a counterattack on evil?
- What wrongs stir me to tears?"

Don't underestimate yourself. Don't underestimate the power of one single step in the right direction. Don't underestimate the power you gain by choosing a worthy enemy. Or someone to love a hundred times more than yourself.

The definition of success: taking a step forward.

CONTEXT: A GODDESS DESCENDED

Shannon and I met at a little college in Oklahoma in 2000. We could not afford it, but my Mom took out a loan at her credit union to make the first month's payment to force me to go. She is quite wise.

My first week, I realized this was where the Mennonites were sending their kids: "Holy hell, this would be a boring place." It was, but I avoided the big mistakes I've seen in young adults. I learned that not losing is sometimes winning.

The definition of success:
taking a step forward.

The first semester of my first senior year, a magnificent goddess descended: a sandy-blonde freshman stepped through those metal band hall doors. Steps change lives. Everything was right. I sat behind her in the trumpet section closely observing the loveliness of her ears, the impeccably manicured feet in those worn-out flip-flops, and the beautiful vibrato from her Selmer Super Action 80 tenor sax. But I was the senior too chicken to speak to that freshman. How would I overcome my fear of rejection and failure?

And so, realizing I wouldn't make a move, a freshman woman asked a senior boy to the Sadie Hawkins weekend dance around the middle of her first semester. And life has never been the same.

And every time I consider that this greatest blessing has come from someone else's belief that I would eventually become a man worth loving, I double down on the thesis that someone else's hope can threaten to revolutionize your life as well. If you just say yes.

WHERE ARE YOU RIGHT NOW?

My business, charitable, and online efforts have brought me into contact with so many fascinating people like you who send me questions about hopelessness, addictions, fears, desires, problems, and regrets. And I get it. Everyone wonders why life isn't any better.

- Did you just turn thirty and now wonder where all the success everyone promised you went?
- Are you middle-aged and wanting to make a grand pivot to find yourself and uncover meaning?
- Do you feel like an imposter when asked to take on a bit of courage?
- Are you wondering how you will find a good woman to love?

I'm writing this in my forties but I'm especially struck by men who are younger than me. Who seem to be seeking a whiff of direction. A model to lead their way. I understand that impulse and want to do my best to offer what help I have.

If you want to copy a plan written by a man who lives in the real world like you, then read on. If you are looking for theories from men who have never really lived, look elsewhere.

So many of you look around at those people with success and fame and think you deserve that as your 16-year-old or 66-year-old self.

But let me tell you the truth: I scrubbed the stainless steel toilets of inmates when I was 15 and was still scrubbing porcelain toilets of corporate interns a decade later when I was 25. Despite having hundreds of employees. That was my career: cleaning crap and finding cash for payroll. I believed in quality so much that I fixed problems myself if I saw something I thought could be better and still overspent on quality staffing. And that desire to do the right thing both helped and held me back.

Between the time I started my first company in college and when I turned 25, I would have done far better financially working at McDonald's than continuing to reinvest and take on debt for the business. The risk was high, and the profits were low. But most men would have quit long before then.

It's the giving up on yourself that perhaps creates your most unforgiving enemy: regret.

But some of us are too stupid to quit, so we finally succeed. Often it's narrow focus and constant failure that produces grit and character. Imagine your future and ask,

- "What is it that I am willing to do eighty hours per week for a decade to change the trajectory of my family forever?
- What do I need to give up doing behind closed doors to become that man who can take on some responsibility outside them?
- What would I do if I knew I could never fail?"

Then why not just do that?

Some of us are too stupid to quit,
so we finally succeed.

THE PROBLEM:
LIFE'S BALANCE

Back home in Texas, arriving from Miami that evening—after the morning of the purging of the Blackberries—I told Shannon about everything. Well, perhaps not everything from the past twenty-four hours, but most everything else from that week. "YeahYeahYeah"—she nodded away everything I said and handed me our one-year-old. She was rightly exhausted and, with a kiss, left me with Emerson.

And now, half a continent away from most of them—merely dealing with messages and "next time you're in the Valley" emails—I could return to life. And as I held Emerson—sleeping against me on the couch—I left their imaginary world and fell back into the real.

I could feel her weight on my chest, could smell that baby's breath which Shannon and I only dreamed of breathing in a year before after losing multiple babies through miscarriages. Emerson's baby's breath was more real than all Miami's promises.

The lives of sex, money, and status most my new friends thought they had the evening before, vanished before they arrived home. My life, however, got more real. And at that point, I decided I wanted to be a real man. Not a fake.

But what did that mean for me in the business world of pride, ambition, and power? What did it mean for a guy like me who loved being home in peace but knew he was ready for a battle? What could that mean for you as you teeter between fake fears and concrete moves?

After all, I still admired the hope and hard work of those drug-fueled leaders in Miami. But without the loneliness, emptiness, and deviated septums. I wanted to be the person who was always optimistic and talked about the future, the man who outworked everyone else, and no one could ever call lazy. But, I needed to figure out a way to lace those together with the magic of our growing family and who I thought I could evolve to become.

But is that what a real man looks like?

THE LESSON:
MURDER THE EVIL

A few years back, the news covered the murder trial of a rancher who admitted to killing a man in Texas. It was not self-defense. He was not insane. Yet that rancher got off.

Based on this information alone, many would be enraged by the lack of justice in not convicting and punishing an admitted killer.

The rancher was the father of a 5-year-old girl. Hearing her screams he found one of his ranch hands in the back of a barn with her, his underwear removed. Pulling the ranch hand off his little girl, the father inflicted multiple blows to the ranch hand's head and body and killed him.

I imagined myself in the same situation as that father. What would I do? I like to think I would be above the anger and hate, and focus on caring for my daughter in that heartache. That I would be compassionate toward her first while calling for the police. The legalist mind of anyone who is not yet a father would tell him that he should control himself and let the justice system play out. It's not worth going to jail and the girl losing her father as well, they would whisper with their weak never-living souls.

But there is something more right in the father's vengeance; something truer about justice and defending your innocents. And yes, here I intend to shock you with the prod of the proper divine conduct which is the opposite of what we were told long ago. I believe it was right, good, and just for the man to take the killing into his own hands. I hoped I would do the same if I were in his situation. His daughter saw—with her own eyes—that true justice mankind never gets to see. And a truer love. Her eyes saw the justice on her perpetrator in a way none of the victims of 9/11 or the Holocaust witnessed. A gift of right love overcoming false lust.

But if I held back and called the police, I would only be half-a-man. And my daughter would see that I was only half of what I could be. And, perhaps, many years later she would marry another half-a-man: weak, safe, and excuse-laden. And they would raise half-sons because that's what she once saw displayed in me as the man who supposedly most rightly loved her. And she would never become her full self, for she only had half-a-father.

The rancher's daughter saw that vile man of lust defeated for good by one true act of a whole man in love. A father who, though like me is imperfect most of the time, then stuns the world once in his life with a moment of wholed perfection. That is all any man can ever hope to do. Life is a string of imperfect moments with the occasional moment of perfection.

> *Life is a string of imperfect moments with the occasional moment of perfection.*

Don't throw one blow when you can throw a hundred against evil. Love is always watching.

The court agreed. Deep down all humanity knows proper hate is the fulfillment of proper love.

> *Hate is not the opposite of love.*
> *Proper hate is the fulfillment of love.*

Imagine what your future would look like if you had one single moment of perfection that could help fulfill your potential.

- One moment where you stood up the funding to sue the sex website that didn't care about minors.
- When you told the boss you were quitting to start your own company.
- Where you pushed down your enemy of rejection and asked the girl to grab a cherry limeade at Sonic.
- Where you stepped into the confrontation instead of walking past.

You could be forever a whole man. Whose presence, years after it happened, would still threaten anyone who thought about whether to verbally attack you or the ones you love today. You would be respected and loved. You would be a man whose friends trust with resources and authority. You would be one of those few men who were ever really alive at some point in his life. You would have met the challenge of a moment truly lived and arise forever a victor.

Lives are only a collection of moments. And a single moment can begin to build a real life. A single step, a winning stride.

THE THEORY:
LOVE REQUIRES HATE

Hate is always wrong when not turned against the negatives of evil, darkness, and chaos. Instead, hate was made for love: a passion created for justice against the wrong, to uphold the right. Hate is not the opposite of love. Rather, proper hate is the fulfillment of love when properly directed.

Now, do not think that I am merely speaking of enemies as people. I speak mainly on fighting the root causes driving the bad men. Those addictions, organizations, wokeist ideologies, and unethical programmatic assaults on our kids in public schools.

Even the Bible commands you to hate what is evil because it is the only way to cling to a little good.

So, hate is for all rightly oriented men because each man must battle injustice. The worse the injustice against goodness and innocence, the more proper his hate and the more right he is in his retribution. If you are seeking a purpose for your life, I offer one here. In the same place where love finds its justice: in the hatred and opposition to the wrong.

> *Love finds its justice in the hatred and opposition to the wrong.*
> _____

We know injustice will look differently:

- The insult of an incompetent boy taking an extra moment's look at your beautiful woman.
- The envy of a forever unemployed healthy woman who mocks the working mom.
- The wrongness of the lower man mocking the wise man is a shadowed blasphemy.

Protection of the innocents under your care requires right-aimed hatred for the detestable. And in a sense all fathers and mothers are called to do that which is not immediately obvious. Yet eternally right.

What does love require of you as a man?

Murder humanities' evil problems and let your loved ones see. They need to know you can be reliable, wise, and loving with the potential to be dangerous to defend them. So do you.

But be advised: I encourage you to become a loving man who can be dangerous. I damn an angry man who claims a bit of love.

And this truer love, which can become dangerous if needed, will look different to all of us.

- For some, it might mean going face-to-face with the bully's dad with your kid watching. Or your mom's abusive third husband.
- Cut the painkillers and let your family see you fight through the withdrawal. Or the alcohol you know you cannot handle.

Only a weak man cannot hate. He therefore can never really love.

But this right-hate is true not just with problems, circumstances, and addictions. But in the literal sense. It is right to go into battle and kill your enemies—not because you hate those in front of you, but because you love those behind you. This love is the motivation for the correct hate. Hate what is evil, cling to what is good.

And this hatred of the wrong is not the opposite of the Christian pursuit, it is the fulfillment of it. We believed the false lies that the nice religious guy was the good guy when he was merely a falsified man in disguise.

But remember that it was the religious who killed Christ and the religious who Christ spoke out against. He was always anti-religion. Truth always is. We will return to Him in later chapters to see how Truth overthrows our weakness despite what we do or don't believe in now.

Only a weak man cannot hate.
He therefore can never really love.

Sometimes our enemies are easy to identify, like that father defending his daughter. But more often enemies hide beneath the surface, like a tumor. Our deepest foes are often a piece of us. Like my fear of rejection in college to ask that freshman girl out.

Our fears make us miss out on life. And love.

YOUR NEXT MOVES

Because you are mortal, you know you can die. But because you are part divine, you suspect you won't. So you are attracted to safety and comfort. Right now, you are pushing off until tomorrow what you should be doing today.

So time becomes your constant nemesis. Time wins if the clock runs out on you. Time doesn't care if you fight or not. Time doesn't care if you love or are loved. So you must maintain urgency in whatever you decide to do. Your standing around must end.

I have faced numerous categories of enemies—religious, organizations, politics, my mind, hostile business partners, my pride, and many others. Through these enemies, I glimpsed my purpose. So can you.

So what should you do right now if you seek a purpose worthy of your only life?

First, unburden yourself from the friends and daily habits you know aren't worth the energy. Pick two friends to give up today. Because a bad friend is far worse than an evil enemy.

A bad friend is far worse than an evil enemy.

Next, choose the highest, most formidable adversary you can and attack. Enemies are more often desires and habits than people.

But what if it's not the right time to fight? You must fight your challenger while you still can—right now. Before you lose the energy you do have. Before your mind fades. Before you get too busy with life and tragedies. Before your decline arrives. And it always will.

But how will you know it's the right enemy? It's often that hidden enemy you ignore. An ideology, organization, philosophy, or evil manifestation. The one you least want to admit exists and never honestly confront. The closer the tougher. And if your foe happens to be hostile to someone you love, you have hope of divine power intervening. Direct your proper hatred in the defense of love. And you will want to live, and love, properly.

Last, you must embrace lavishness on the extremes of love and evil. Aim to ward off the evil addictions you hide. Send a hundred bullets when just one might do. Make a hundred cold calls to overcome that fear holding you back from rejection. These acts prepare you not just to become a man who fights but a man who can one day love.

Whatever your worthy challenge is, put in a hundred reps today. Pick the most obvious and physical act you least want to do. What you least want to do is often what you most need to do next. You can plan as you work but don't delay.

> *"Those who lack the courage will always find a philosophy to justify it."*
> — ALBERT CAMUS

If you are a good man who rightly loves, and has a big enough challenge, you will have all the resources and energy you need. But you will not rest because you are living out a real purpose. And as you fight with all you have, you gain the hope of a higher help. A stronger hope than any man with a million friends. And that is the beginning of a real life if you want one. Life is in the steps.

The purpose of light is to invade the darkness. The purpose of good is to invade the evil. Pick a problem. Choose an adversary too difficult to beat as you are now. You'll grow stronger as you love and learn. What problem breaks your heart?

You'll know how to do it, just like Alexander the Great did. And no one had a more formidable enemy than this man who fought and conquered the world. We'll spend the next two chapters showing his pivot: from deceiver to role model. You and I are quite a bit like Alexander if you get past the wealth and military. We make the same mistakes and are restored in the same manner.

It's not winning that makes a man good, but fighting for someone worth loving.

Pick a worthy problem and don't hold back.

TOOL: TEN URGENCY ACCELERATORS

So what needs to be done next? What is the fastest way to experience the needed changes? How can you muster the resources and urgency to battle a worthy enemy?

Download this tool for free at **RICKWALKER.COM/9STEPS**

PAIR A:
OUR INTERNAL DECLINE AND ASCENT

> "If we were stronger, we might be less tenderly treated. If we were braver, we might be sent, with far less help, to defend far more desperate posts in the great battle."
>
> — C.S. LEWIS

"Alexander Visits the Sage Plato in his Mountain Cave" by Basawa is a vibrant 17th-century Indian miniature painting. It depicts Alexander the Great seeking wisdom from Plato, who resides in a secluded cave. The artwork, part of The Metropolitan Museum of Art's collection, exemplifies detailed Mughal artistry and storytelling.

Courtesy: The Met, New York City.

View this art in full color and resolution at RickWalker.com/9steps

STEP

2

AIM HIGH.
AIMING LOW
IS THE ONLY SIN.

*To look up you must
first look back.*

THE SET-UP:
I WALKED AWAY IN DEFEAT

Aiming low is the only sin.

By 2017, I had founded multiple businesses. Launches are intoxicating: spinning up a brand, website, and strategy, hiring the right folks, building processes, experimenting with marketing mix, and finding that critical mass of clients. And so, by my late 30s, I had a large federal contracting business managing complex real estate projects and construction projects for the Federal Government—now working in six states. I also had a commercial real estate consulting business that advised wealthy clients on buying and selling their commercial properties, managed corporate campuses, and negotiated hundreds of real estate transactions on behalf of investors. I also owned the majority of a private equity company that invested in other companies across real estate and public-private equities. There were many entities, but they functioned together in the commercial real estate space.

I had everything I ever dreamed of. I had scaled multiple multi-million-dollar businesses, one up to 400 employees, was Chairman of a major nonprofit, which we had already scaled from 800 team members in 2007 to 2,300 team members in 2017—across 50 countries, and a voracious board schedule with work I enjoyed as a volunteer for other great organizations. An impressive wife and three darling daughters, I spent half my day in the nonprofit world and the other eight hours per day in my businesses. We jaunted to Cabo, Vail, Aspen, Manhattan, and Florida for weeks at a time most years. Life was full.

And I tell you this not because I earned all of it, but because I was entrusted with it as a divine steward. Yes, I worked hard, but just as that freshman girl asked me out as a senior in college, so too I am merely the recipient of the blessing by a thousand hands: family, partners, and employees. And probably mostly by my Mom's praying hands. I am not a self-made man. But I do want to cast a vision of what these 9 Steps offer for you as well.

That year, as Chairman of a complex global organization, we suspected potential fraud in one of the key employee's family members, likely unknowingly aided by an insider, and asked three CPAs to take a closer look with permission of the governing committee (which oversaw audit and controls). A month later, the findings concluding potentially improper transactions were presented to their committee and leaked to the 30-person board.

When it became apparent the board would not even discuss or refer the transactions dating back a decade to yet another auditor for a fourth confirmatory opinion, let alone address the parties involved, I realized I could either blow up the organization, which positively impacted millions of lives while employing thousands or walk away. So, after hiring an attorney to draft a 50-page letter on ethics and responsibility for the entire board and considering my confidentiality commitments, I attached a resignation letter and moved on.

I preferred a clean heart and dirty hands over association with the dirty spines of cowards. They were nice people, just cowards. And I would not succumb to allowing even the appearance of deception in leading a group of capable people for whom I was responsible. I would not commit the lowering sin of avoiding difficult conversations to allow comfortable mediocrity to persist. I would not allow my lower desire to remain in control and make demands to overcome my higher duty as a man to do the noble act where I could. I would not partake in a lie.

But I also would not allow my hand to tear down much of my work. I would not call ignorant, cowardly men my enemies just because they are mistaken. And I certainly would not sabotage my sweat and charitable financial investments to prove I could win a legal battle. Never destroy the world you conquer if it cannot destroy you.

Truth is worth discovering, but mind the damage when the enemy is merely an idiot. My walking away washed away a decade of my favorite relationships. Aiming high also means avoiding unworthy enemies. And cowards.

Aiming high means avoiding unworthy enemies.

If you are composed in life's storms, the 9 Steps in this book will compound in your favor.

And I realize that many of my experiences are highly unique and you're trying to figure out how they relate to your life. I encourage you to see the principles despite the size, success, and circumstances. But the reason I share much of this is to highlight that the falls are further down the higher you climb up.

MY STORM CLOUDS

But 2017 was not over. After walking away from a decade of work at the global charity, Hurricane Harvey hit Houston in August that year with 50 inches of rain in many parts of the region. After the storms subsided, we slept with no water in our street. But we had heard water would be coming from a dam an hour north of us and down the San Jacinto toward us in the morning. So, I slept on the floor at the lowest point of the house to wake up if the waters rose. Lake Houston was a couple hundred yards from our home. And in a day, 16,000 homes around the lake flooded from waters that rained an hour upstream.

A few hours later, Shannon, the girls, and the dog stepped from our foyer directly into a friend's boat docked on our front porch. They carried a couple of overnight bags in heavy-duty trash sacks. I told them to go get to high ground at our friend's home, and I'd join them later.

We lived on a cul-de-sac of amazing seniors, so I stayed back. To wade the chest-high sludge. I had to get around to them all, making sure their electricity and gas were off, helping them move their valuables upstairs, moving pianos, and trying to convince them to leave in boats.

Just before night fell and with electricity off, I watched as rescuers pulled the final neighbors from their homes. I left after that on a boat to meet my family. As I departed, stalled boats with rutters broken off from brick mailboxes sat lining the street. The yards where my kids played were covered in filthy water. Only the tops of many cars still visible. And as the boat let me off at the only dry place—the park which was now a boat launch filled with trailers—I gathered into my buddy's truck to get to the house where my girls were. He told me the flood waters took out every restaurant, grocery store, and shop for a mile. Eight feet of water in our Starbucks that had only been open for a month. The community was underwater and under-prepared.

By the end of the next day, my entire first floor—its contents and construction materials—sat on the front lawn in a giant pile. Refrigerators were duct-taped shut to keep the rotten takeout inside from spilling out. Even the doors, frame, and trim had to be tossed, and openings had to be boarded up to keep critters out.

Like a decaying molar or alcoholic date, we had to cut everything away which could come back to destroy our well-being.

The floods devastated our entire community. So, over the next few days, friends and I would gut (or muck out) five other homes. Water wicks up walls, so by the fifth day, a home with a two-foot flood works upward to four feet in many homes. And since drywall is in eight-foot sheets, instead of cutting at four and a half feet with three feet of waste, they demolish the drywall up to eight feet to lay a full sheet of drywall back.

I had underestimated the difficulty and expense of rebuilding by a factor of four. But for now, we were still optimistic that this would be a few weeks of inconvenience.

I should have renewed our flood policies, so the $650,000 to replace and rebuild was out of our pocket. I just didn't think about renewing the policy and didn't recall a renewal notice coming.

Shannon and I were in it together. We enjoyed picking out new furniture and finishes. Though stressful and unplanned, it was a little like designing a new house. We lived upstairs for eight months during construction.

But sometimes a man picking out drapes needs to pick a fight.

The next month, September, my largest company lost its largest client. We had completed a multi-year contract for work they no longer needed, and we had worked ourselves out of a job.

MY RUN FOR U.S. CONGRESS

Within sixty days of our home's demise, our long-time U.S. Representative in Congress announced he was retiring. That was a big setback in a seniority-led House because our community relied on him to get our federal remediation and engineering funding to rebuild and protect us from future disasters.

And not noticing any other competent individuals willing to do so, I jumped into what ended up being one of the most expensive Congressional primaries ever. Over a 120-day campaign period, nine candidates squandered nearly $15 million.

I thought my pride could cover up for my weak political chops, and personal and financial struggles of that year. So here I was about to embark on a great adventure while still aiming low and inward on myself.

I had a little personal cash, but not much considering the task. For years, we had given up to 60% of our income to charities, leaving little liquidity. If you look up my publicly available Federal Campaign Financial Disclosure Report filing for 2017, you will notice my Schedule A assets totaled between

$7 million and $31 million. It's a wide range, but most of it was illiquid and inaccessible.

Even still, I spent over half my time fundraising and only raised around $100,000. This was due to the federal limits, which were $2,200 per donor then. The remaining $500,000 or so we spent came out of my pocket.

I arrived at the leased campaign offices in a run-down office building most mornings around 6 or 7, after being up late the night before. Shannon would arrive each morning after getting the girls to school, to start the volunteers writing cards and making calls. We were generally there together most days for several hours before I'd leave for a lunch presentation or debate. But I would not see our three daughters very much unless we were blockwalking on Saturday mornings. I was out before they were up, and in well after they went to bed.

There were a few verbal attacks in person, mostly by me as the aggressor, thousands of TV ads, scrambles to pick up endorsements of no-name hacks, morning strategy meetings, block walks, and, of course, polling.

My ego was ablaze in Alexandrian fashion, primarily due to the debates and the press. I got to talk about myself all day and night—the narcissist's dream. And even better, I could do it to help others. The perfect cover-up.

I debated eight savvy candidates nine times. These debates required us to brush up on the esoteric platforms in which the hosting groups were most interested. The policies remain the same, but the rhetoric varies strategically. The claims of competence from some of these candidates were laughable. Everyone spoke like they would have the authority to make whatever changes they wished for the world. Want a wall? No problem. Want to close the IRS? Sure. We promised anything for the allegiance of a few loyal supporters. We acted like we were gods and conquerors, and wanted others to campaign for us as such. In reality, we would have nearly zero authority.

Like mine, Alexander's brutal arrogance pressed ahead to defeat his foes in his many hard-fought campaigns.

You and I have so much in common with Alexander the Great. And here I want to show you how he also falls so that you can see yourself in the next chapter as he soars.

The eagle must leap out of the safety to rise. So must you.

ALEXANDER THE LOW

Upon conquering the entire known world, Alexander the Great's epithet read: "A tomb now suffices for him, for whom the world was not enough."

The entire universe was his enemy. He won, but it was never enough. He conquered, yet his desires still searched. He was never satisfied. He filled his mind and heart with lowly physical treasures and trinkets of the world. He aimed low in his campaigning, just like me.

When we assume a higher place, such as being superior to Christ, Zeus, or Krishna, we make an ambitious blunder that proves our vain pride. We, too, say even the whole world isn't enough for us. Are you ever really satisfied?

Aristotle tutored Alexander and mentored him for succession after King Philip II. Imagine the expectations for someone Aristotle mentored to be a king.

Alexander sought fame with deception as his weapon—deception aimed against his men as he claimed to be divine. You and I commit a similar sin: wanting to set up on our own and be god-like.

And there we fail to realize there is no one else left to rescue us from our evil if no one is higher on whom to depend. There is no one else to learn from as an example. No one higher to aim at. So we aim low.

THE PLOT: ALEXANDER'S ASCENT TO POWER

Alexander's infamy began when he was young. His father, King Philip II, ruled and warred victoriously. Philip beat back the most brutal opponents around. He dominated both the Balkans and Greece and saved Macedonia from near ruin in his campaign.

Weaponizing his effective leadership of men, Philip built an army of seasoned and speeded warriors. Like Nazi Germany's famed Panzer divisions, speed was a decisive advantage in warfare even two millennia ago.

Step forward with strength and speed.

In BC 336, the 47-year-old King Phillip II attended the theater of Aegae for a celebration due to the attendance by both Greeks and Macedonians. It highlighted their loyalty to and appreciation of him. But Philip's bodyguard, Pausanias, was not as loyal.

History tells us that as the king entered, Pausanias stormed out of the team of bodyguards and toward Philip. From under the darkness of the guard's cloak, a dagger flashed, only to return to the darkness of Philip's kingly ribs. The assassin Pausanias ran away, but his foot hung up on a tree's root during his escape. Pausanias' collegiate bodyguards killed Pausanias within moments, as Alexander's father-king Philip passed.

Heir apparent, the twenty-one-year-old Alexander was crowned within hours.

Under the influence of his mother, and recalling his father's instruction, Alexander ordered the next two rivals to the throne murdered. If threats do not contain opportunities, they must be destroyed. These Macedonian murders were a mere act of Machiavellian practicality.

> *If threats do not contain opportunities, they must be destroyed.*

Rumors arose that Alexander was the mastermind behind his own father's murder. He was the most to benefit and would have the power to conceal. Nevertheless, the opportunity presented itself to a calculating man.

THE ANTI-LESSON: THE WINNING LIE

Alexander rose to speak to his men upon his ascent, as I had in many campaign speeches. He lied. He told them that King Philip II was not his father. Not satisfied to be the son of the most formidable king. Insufficient for him to be most dominant. Wanting a better name so he might become more triumphant. Desiring more power than what his real father offered. I'll build the wall.

Alexander began a rumor his father was Zeus, the seed of Jupiter and son of the sky god. Alexander, like Hercules and Achilles, claimed to be the god-man on earth. And it worked. Lies often do work for a time. But only if you have the status, and campaign support, to maintain them as truths.

Claiming to be the son of Zeus, he stole a bit of his divinity, despite the command: "thou shall not use the name of Zeus your god in vain." This is the essence of the primary commands given to the Jews, Indians, and the ancient Platonists: Do not think you are better than you are. Mind the gap between yourself and the gods. They are holy for a reason.

His mother, Olympias, also benefited from her false conjugal connection to the thunder god when she commanded this army after Alexander's death. Mary's union and immaculate conception likewise propelled her to eternal grandeur in Catholic theology due to her son's divine paternity.

The story you tell matters. Your story is the brand and identity others see. And eventually, you may believe yourself—whether lies or truths.

THE PROBLEM: TRUTH AND SUCCESS

How do you become the type of man Alexander was with the influence and success but without the deception?

It was a similar question I had asked after my experience with the drug-fueled CEOs in Miami: How do we achieve optimism without false desires? How can I make the work I do last despite the messiness of incompetence surrounding it?

I wanted to discover the balance between success and ethics. I have always been told there are trade-offs if you want to be relevant. But what did that mean? And why was it usually unsuccessful people who said it?

We men use this trade-off fallacy as an excuse for laziness and noncommitment. We hide under this cloak of perceived goodness. We avoid responsibility not realizing we murder our meaning.

> *When we avoid responsibility we murder our meaning.*

It's most often the book-smart but spineless men who claim their lack of success is due to their virtue and humility. They then play the victim card, the tortured saint, or the family man as an excuse for why they aimed at mediocrity and hit it. It's those low-aiming men who lie to themselves with the opposite lie of Alexander: to blame fate instead of taking responsibility for their own futures.

Responsibility means risk. Risk you might lose. Risk you might get a dagger out of the cloak. Risk that you will have to conspire with the gods to maintain power.

You should consider the future when acting in your present. You will be successful if you blend passion, right living, risk-taking, and competency to do something worthwhile and unselfish. You will not need that lie that you are in control and invincible and perfect. Likewise, you will not need those excuses the weak men give for their failures. You are strong and will hit fate squarely on the nose like a man.

Alexander is scheming and politicking, which ends in a lie to advance his cause. So your question about Alexander should be very similar to my question about those Silicon Valley playboy titans: How can I aim high with my life?

But it will take knowing the difference between a worthy enemy to fight and a false enemy to avoid. You must pick your battles, while always choosing the high, noble, and true way.

First, ask what needs to be done and what's right. The most alluring battles can sometimes be a mirage, tempting your ego to tear down your own work.

MY CAMPAIGN, MY RULES

U.S. Congressional Districts contained between 700,000 and 800,000 residents. As one of the two candidates who could afford proper statistical polling, my advisors said no one would win the 9-candidate campaign outright, with over 50%, and it would be won in a run-off. So, the goal was to get into the top two to reach the run-off in March. For weeks, a very wealthy socialite and I polled the top two. She knew it, and I knew it. The mixed-mode polling, from the end of January with early voting to begin a little over a month later, had me with 44% on an informed ballot—with 37% undecided. The nearest competitor had 11%.

A month before the March primary, my polling indicated the socialite was approaching 50%. I had to do something drastic. I had hired professionals to run the campaign—strategists and managers—but I was the candidate. And in my ignorance, I started calling the shots. I chose my whims over the experience of my staff.

My name was on the campaign, so if I was going to pay for nearly everything and outwork the professionals, I decided I'd run it like I wanted. So, against the advice of my experienced team, I began ordering TV spots and using vendors I knew.

This belief that I knew more than the people who had been there a thousand times before was my taking another apple bite of that deadly tree of knowledge and rebellion. I should have followed their advice, for they could see further than I could.

Many people are keyboard warriors and hide behind their screens. But because of my days telemarketing and going door-to-door to start my company, I was willing to say the tough things face-to-face, which made many uncomfortable. But it gave me a superpower after the race because I learned to enjoy feeling my poise while seeing my enemies' unease. I developed the superpower to convert a counter-party's discomfort into my strength.

There is a difference between vulnerability and cowardice. One is divine. One is evil.

I went on a tear of in-person tear-downs of the socialite as she hit 50%. Villainizing her for various nuanced infractions. She wasn't bad, she was just rich and inexperienced. And I had just gotten rebuffed months prior by a group of 30 rich, incompetent people I had put on my own board from which I walked away.

Fearing those attacks were not enough, I escalated things to a nuclear level. Here, it became my mission not to win but for her to lose. So, I paid another three professional block walkers to visit constituents with a message of "anyone but her." The weak think victory is the defeat of others.

> *The weak think victory is the defeat of others.*

I then hired the top polling company in America, out of D.C., to test the specific wording for televised attack ads. They polled everything imaginable to determine the highest percentage of her current supporters who would retract their support if they knew one of these facts. Everything they tested was true—we didn't let them try out lies. I was looking for one point on her Achilles' high heel.

And they found it.

And so, an unnamed cocky son-of-a-bitch whose wife was running subcontractors during the day to rebuild his destroyed house with his kids in tow and her wrangling his volunteers at night, ignoring his cratering businesses while only talking about himself for months, spent all their personal savings to run over 1,000 TV spots to destroy the campaign of a very nice lady who had given millions to great causes over the years.

Not to win. But to destroy.

Then she countered. Two oversized postcards were sent to nearly 800,000 the following week. She even sent them to nonvoters and the other party just for fun—twice. Well played. One accused me of being anti-jobs when, in fact, I campaigned on creating more jobs than all other candidates combined. The other mailer called me Satan on a poster held up by an angry mob. I never heard her radio ads, but I heard they were well-produced. I had to admire good work.

Sometimes a worthy enemy is worth more than any friend. And sometimes you pick a false enemy and they destroy you.

THE VOTES ARE CAST

Our friends were incredible: placing signs, working security at events, hand writing letters, and making calls to likely voters—we are so thankful. They hosted breakfasts, coffees, and dinners for me to meet their friends. There are far too many to mention, but dozens who gave up weeks of their lives. We will never forget their love for us.

Most of the volunteers were Shannon's friends through the swim team, PTA, and various other friend groups. Don't mess with stay-at-home Moms—they're all business. Most of my friends lived in other parts of Houston, yet traveled to help or host fundraisers.

On election night, we hosted around 100 of our hardest-working supporters for a victory party. Victory parties are what watch parties used to be, but for vain people who boast about what they can do, like me and Alexander. As the results began pouring in, we were optimistic.

I was still thinking of my Grandma who had just passed, and thought it would honor her to win.

Candle-warmed stainless steel trays of shrimp skewers, fries, and chicken fingers sat against the restaurant windows, with a small adjacent cash bar pumping out hydration. The restaurant owners worked the party themselves in entrepreneurial fashion. A few younger kiddos ran around with mine, and a handful of preteens sat on the front porch swing.

But the adults were glued to their phones, continuously refreshing the county elections reporting website. The results began streaming in at seven when the polls closed, but the full results wouldn't come until midnight. I ignored the initial results, which arrived by neighborhood (called precincts) because each of the hundreds of precincts had a certain tendency that was too difficult to track. I wanted to mingle and show appreciation instead of staring at my phone. I was in a room of friends better than I could ever become.

Then around nine o'clock, the most embarrassing moment of my life hit my phone the one time I decided to look.

My parents lived four hours away in Corpus Christi and watched a national news broadcast on election night. They watched political news all night every night, but this night, they were paying special attention. They loved politics, but given that my Mom's mother had been dying the past few months, they couldn't drive the four hours to Houston to help much at that time. My parents are amazing.

Then...

My phone.

A text from them.

A photo showed *NBC National News*.

My headshot.

The number 3% under it.

Not only were they projecting I lost but worse.

Annihilated.

On national news.

That text message continued a chain of events in my life which I later learned the ancient Stoics called a clusterfuck.

Now, I had to breathe in a crowded room of people who all expected me to be competitive. Matt, my campaign manager, called the crowd together to recite Teddy Roosevelt's 1910 Man in the Arena speech to give me a moment to collect my thoughts:

> "It is not the critic who counts; not the man who points out how the strong man stumbles, or where the doer of deeds could have done them better. The credit belongs to the man who is actually in the arena, whose face is marred by dust and sweat and blood; who strives valiantly; who errs, who comes short again and again, because there is no effort without error and shortcoming; but who does actually strive to do the deeds; who knows great enthusiasms, the great devotions; who spends himself in a worthy cause; who at the best knows in the end the triumph of high achievement, and who at the worst, if he fails, at least fails while daring greatly, so that his place shall never be with those cold and timid souls who neither know victory nor defeat."

And with the word *defeat* still ringing in the air I weakly rose to speak of my defeat in the very moment of it. Exposed and alone, like my daughter Emerson in her ballet recital en pointe.

But not lovely. Humiliated more than ever.

"It's said blood's for a moment, but friendship for a lifetime. Shannon and

I are deeply thankful for every one of you, friends. Your careful attention. Your energy. Your presence. It's said that all bad things can work together to create good. Sitting here just a minute ago, I didn't buy it. I wanted to say it, though. But now, standing, I can now see. I see the goodness in each of your faces reflected on me in my defeat. At this very moment, I see a collection of brave friends who believed in me. Not just a belief in our victory, but a belief in our shared vision of a family-first movement in a floodless and healed community. And so, I want to thank each of you from the bottom of my heart. Shannon and the girls especially."

Both the socialite and I self-imploded. All the attack ads caused mutual destruction at our own hands. She fell to third place, and I took fourth with 7% at the final tally. The planned attack worked. It caused her to lose over half her supporters. The problem, however, is that those supporters didn't move to me. Instead, they almost entirely moved to fourth place, a young military hero now entering the run-off.

I waited until everyone left the restaurant, then headed home. Throwing that politician's red tie into the passenger's seat, I called to congratulate the winners who made it into the run-off. They were listed on the polling weeks earlier at 3% and 1% informed polling. From that moment, I began to doubt myself.

THE AFTER-PARTY

I lost the campaign on national news and delivered my loser's speech in epic embarrassment less than an hour before I pulled into our construction debris-filled driveway.

When I returned home from the victory-turned-defeat party to the wife and kids I had ignored for months, I hadn't considered their set expectations. Shannon planned to live between Houston and D.C.—school, nanny, and homes. She had worked so hard, and I messed it up by going negative in my campaign.

I had recklessly run a plow through that farmer's daughter's heart.

And in that guest bedroom upstairs of our torn-up home, she tore me down when she said she was done with me. I didn't blame her.

After all, I had ignored her and the girls for four months—perhaps years. I used them for campaign events and ads. Between the campaign and the house being uninsured, in a matter of weeks I wasted over a million dollars of our personal money while ignoring my struggling businesses. All the while, I did nothing but talk about myself while I thought of myself.

I was done with me too. Not suicide, but fed-up with my Alexandrian self-focus. The political game. The pandering. The exhibition.

As long as I was looking down on others, I could not see what was above. My ego became my master. I had aimed low, instead of high.

That night in complete exhaustion, I slept without any hope. Shannon and I hung on in miserable matrimony. My largest client in my other larger business went through bankruptcy before we lost them in May of 2019. Both my major businesses had lost nearly 75% of their revenues as I returned to work months later to assess the damage my absence had caused.

It had been a brutal year of losing.

THE THEORY: WHO ARE YOU BECOMING?

I've built and destroyed some great brands and campaigns. And nice people.

Building a brand means telling a story.

Life is a story. And most stories are never relevant. But perhaps looking through a great enough story, we can glimpse the source of true relevance. A false story once proved relevant in Alexander's case. But what about us? What story are you telling yourself? What fake story are you trying to sell to the others around you?

If the story of my very self is a lie, my entire life will run amok. I become uncenterable. I destroy myself as I destroy others. And if I'm not made whole I'll become a hole—caverning in on myself. Likewise Alexander's cavernous heart sought a greater story to fill his need for relevance and purpose. Even if it was a lie. Lies weigh all men down.

Lies weigh all men down.

He didn't want just one country, or two. Not three. You will not be happy with just one Ferrari. But all of them. This was the discontentment of Alexander: his search for worth in pursuit of the crowns of men. Blaise Pascal's judgment of mankind speaks of all of us:

"Inside each of us, there sits the Infinite hole."

Your infinite worth was not made to be enveloped by the finite world.

You were made for something beyond this world, made not for the visible but by an invisible mold. And the best molds sometimes look like wooden crosses. The best men may even look like losers, perhaps as if they have already died. The highest aim sometimes looks like defeat.

> *The highest aim
> sometimes looks like defeat.*

Our—you, me, Alexander—tombstone epitaph is the very lesson of purpose we spend our lives searching for, only coming hours too late. It may say: Father. Mother. Daughter. Son. Candidate. Loser.

But it's not what you say, or what others call you, but who you become that makes a worthy life. Our purpose is so evident, yet we too ruin our world with our pride. And comfort.

> *It's not what you say but who you become
> that makes a worthy life.*

Augustine of Hippo said ambitions can be met through a relationship with the divine. You are only complete and satisfied once you attain the highest ideal, integrity, intellect, and imagination.

The great thinkers of philosophies and ancient religions demanded that you take an imaginative leap just beyond the shore of your comfort—a leap out of the lies we tell ourselves.

Only leaps can veto voids.

THE WISEST MIND

When you and I look around, we get caught up in comparing ourselves to others. Looking back to my giving and pursuits before 2017 with new eyes, I realized I pursued superiority by comparison. Weak men like me lived by comparison:

More money than him.

More knowledgeable than her.
Everlasting fame.
More likes.

But that is not wisdom. Nor a good life. You and I must look further. But how far?

I believe the wisest mind looks into the most distant future for the most valued reward, which can only be purchased with the currency of the present.

The wisest mind looks into the most distant future for the most valued reward, which can only be purchased with the currency of the present.

The death threats, national embarrassment, and desire to escape created a change in me. I had been thinking too low—in terms of years and decades. Periods too short for quality decisions.

I decided to think longer. Tweets last minutes, podcasts last days, and blogs last weeks. But ideas and books can outlast nations. And perhaps I would one day share a worthy idea—or story—that may endure forever.

Are you thinking too short?

So identify that wisest strategy by identifying the following three elements in that formula:

1. The most distant future (the eternal)
2. The most valuable reward (the highest aim)
3. The currency of the present (your time)

* * *

Oh, and the campaign results. Following an appearance on Saturday Night Live, one candidate took all the energy from the other. Overcoming a life-threatening injury and the loss of an eye from an IED, his eyepatch and elegant articulation had caught their attention. A few weeks later, a much younger, hipper, and savvier former Navy SEAL became the U.S. Representative-elect for Charlie Wilson's Texas Congressional District Two. I was happy to see I was beat by a better man for the job. Dan and Tara

Crenshaw have become close friends to Shannon and I in the years since. I am inspired by Dan's love for cats and pocket-sized dogs.

And from what I now know about Congress, and what my family has been through since, my winning would have been a curse for me. But it took me years to realize that.

> *"Each of us must turn inward and destroy in himself all that he thinks he ought to destroy in others."*
>
> ETTY HILLESUM

Not all those who are against you are worthy enemies. Sometimes the villain you want to defeat is a hero trying to save you from a cursed future you can't see.

YOUR NEXT MOVES

Now it's your turn to give some answers and perhaps to take a step or two into your future.

- So, how will you aim higher?
- How will you avoid the curses you can't see?
- How will you begin looking ahead to life's grander initiatives while struggling with everyday work?
- How will you get over defeats?
- How will you begin to look up and take some advice from people who know better than you?

You must decide which winning lessons and theories to keep and which losers to toss overboard. Let me offer you three sorts of possible places you can begin:

- challenging mentors,
- books, and
- nobility.

Let me explain. Your mentors and advisors bring the sharpening you need to be deadly. Once he ascended to power, Alexander never had honest advisors sitting around the table who would tell him the whole truth or disagree with him to flesh out his thinking. They were speaking to a god, after all.

*Your mentors and advisors bring the sharpening
you need to be deadly.*

Ray Dalio, founder of Bridgewater, currently the world's largest hedge fund, is somewhat of a modern-day philosopher-king. He writes about models of thought and world order while understanding the interplay between systems, which is the arbitrage of ideas.

Dalio advocates triangulation when making a tough decision. He brings the three smartest people on a topic around the same table and presents them with a problem he's thinking through. After a round of their thoughts, he begins to push back a little to test their ideas.

Value is discovered in disagreement. And friction.

As Dalio pushes back against these three people, often mentors, he quiets down to listen to the interchange.

He observes. He humbles himself.

For you, to observe contains the idea of your humility of attention. Observing your mentors carries the idea of rejecting the new in favor of the proven. Second only to meditation, somewhat like prayer, triangulation is likely Dalio's most valuable decision-making tool.

I began to find something like this in the Koch M.B.M. (Market-Based Management system) through the concept of challenge sessions. The Koch Industries process of challenge sessions is a different approach, and valuable. I have been very fortunate to be mentored by a former leader of a Koch business, Kyle Vann, who worked directly with its founder, Charles Koch, in developing and training the various leaders of the Koch billion-dollar businesses, on this M.B.M. process of what it means to lead within the Koch empire. Koch is the second largest privately held company in the United States.

Wouldn't you imagine retraining dozens of war-hardened executives of multi-billion-dollar companies is a Herculean challenge?

But these leaders know challenge is merely refinement. Refinement contains the seed of perfection toward an ideal. It can propel you or stop you.

Like a worthy enemy, your challenge is your refinement toward an ideal future.

*A challenge can propel you
or stop you.*

Keep your future in mind, envision the life you're aiming for, and ask yourself,

- "What challenges have I faced and how did I respond?
- Had I waited another day or two, would I have been better positioned?
- How can I stop one ignoble action today, and replace it with a higher and nobler action which will make my tomorrow one percent better?
- What am I afraid to say to my boss to improve the company?"

Your future is overbrimming with opportunities, which come in the form of refinement and friction—and each hurts.

So you need to name your future self you want to see one day. I did. Pick three traits you wish others to consider when they hear your name. And if you want me to choose for you now, I will. "Responsible. Truthful. Relentless."

For example, "Passionate, Disciplined, Wise" is my desired future state, and all my self-improvement efforts are focused on it.

Name your future self.
You need an ideal to aim yourself.

Like Koch and Dalio, you must attack the idea at hand—the option, course, or trade-off—to see if it can stand on its own. And trustworthy mentors and advisors to do the same.

Interestingly enough, as a time-bound man, the quickest way for you to judge an idea is to go back to the oldest and wisest. The older the sage, the quicker the solution. Allow them to judge the idea for you.

The older the sage,
the quicker the solution.

Charles Koch gave the Koch business leaders books on philosophy, political states, and behavioral economics to expand their thinking because this billionaire sage understood that the proper arbitrage and convergence of ideas will aim, not distract, a man higher.

But he is also a sage manufacturer.

Kyle is a world-class sage-like philosopher himself. His humility and intellectual honesty in knowing he was receiving wisdom from a mentor above him allowed him to catch the stream of wisdom pouring down to him. And I like to think a few drops fell to me.

He once told me he was given two weeks to read a book—*Human Action* by Austrian economist Ludwig von Mises—while he was the leader of a massive trading business. Called the most outstanding defense of capitalism ever written, it provided an understanding of motivations and behavioral theory, which the communists insisted was flawed. The book was over 1,100 pages long, and he returned in two weeks prepared to discuss it. He understood his mentor knew best. So if understanding the collision of domains is important enough for a self-made billionaire to distract his CEO from running one of his multi-billion dollar companies for two weeks to read, it might be vital for you as well.

The world inundates you with a million new books, podcasts, songs, and blogs. You need the older sages to beat up the ideas of the younger men to see how big a boy they really are: Intellectually. Emotionally. Especially imaginatively.

Savvy billionaires use these confrontational meetings to beat up an idea to see how well it stands. They have a confrontation, and they poke and prod an idea to figure out how to do something better. They must be Socratically critical of the idea to flesh it out during these sessions. You, too, must seek not to look right but to do right.

I hope you will adapt these tools of arbitrage, debate, and reflection, and pair them with deep thinking in solitude.

But what about the sages of history? Shouldn't they still get a say? Shouldn't Plato get a say in a world where Taylor Swift receives one?

Second, you have to reflect on what's happened in humanity's past and in history and evaluate how various strategies have turned out for similarly situated people.

Sometimes, like a man in a mental fog, you cannot think as fully and deeply as you would like. This is where old books and dead wise men can help. This model of mentors, books, and asking for advice is often a way back out of the haze for me.

You should be a voracious learner while you can. You've got to become a student of various modes of thought—systems across a wide variety of civilization and faith systems. Yes, to look up, you must look back. But look up at what?

When I read Dante's Inferno, written in Florentine Italian, I must understand the context of Virgil, the Pagan Poet from BC 70, and why he is leading Dante through Hell but is not in Hell himself. The Roman Virgil there looks back, and up, to Aristotle and Plato and the great Greek philosophers.

All great men follow greater men.

You will discover everything worth thinking about is found in more remarkable men of the past. And nearly all the truly great men have been dead for centuries.

When reflecting on your future and your books, think in centuries and millennia, not years and decades. Only centuries can prove ideas and men to be true.

*To look up requires you
to look back.*

And finally, direct your energy toward something worthy. Something high. Something noble. And nothing is more kingly than acting nobly toward the innocents you see. Nobility is never in a rush. It is never flustered. Nobility sleeps on its decisions.

And there is nothing more noble than sacrificial love.

So, if you want to be a man who holds his head high, and seeks the most for his life, you must look up by looking back to the wisdom of the past.

But there are so many options, how can you discover what is true and right? How can you dedicate your life to something worthy?

In Step 1, I asked you to choose one worthy enemy to fight. And be savage. No excuses. Win at all costs. This will give you the clarity and energy to have a worthwhile pursuit.

This is the life that is the antithesis of the self-proclaimed "good" man who says he will not seek glory, power, or money. Using false goodness, this "good" man becomes corrupt because he squanders his very life. No man who aimed low ever really lived. He who squanders his life deserves hell.

However, if you have an enemy to fight, you somehow receive energy—energy to look up and back, to dialog, to think. To find a mentor at just the right moment.

Read the great books of Dostoevsky, Dante, and Milton to learn the enduring reasons why mankind functions and not just the how.

And if you have the energy from a worthy problem you are genuinely fighting to solve and a higher purpose—perhaps even divine—you can really begin to do something.

If you learn, debate, and take noble action in campaigns, you begin to take on king-like attributes. This is how Alexander the Great moved from an empty lie-focused campaigner to the role model we will discuss in the next chapter. Yes, fulfillment and redemption are possible for you, me, candidates who attack unworthy enemies, and even Alexander. And we will see how, like you and me, he had a huge amount of help to get there once he took one specific step away from his lowness.

If you look down and take advice from the average men of today and the political hacks, you will end up nothing. And forgotten.

So look back to the greats to aim your only life at something higher than yourself. Aim to discover one high unifying truth to build your life around. For that is where true life lives.

Aiming low is the only sin.

TOOL: 8 RULES OF EFFECTIVE MEN

Only the effective man can be lavish when he needs to be so. The famed business professor Peter Drucker was the master coach, and over time, he set the gold standard for what makes an Effective Executive. Here, I want to adapt his 8 rules to tell you what I see Effective Men usually doing at work and in leading others.

Download this tool for free at **RICKWALKER.COM/9STEPS**

This exquisite textile, *Four Episodes in the Story of Hercules*, showcases mythological scenes woven with intricate detail, capturing Hercules' legendary feats as a god-man. Vibrant hues and elaborate motifs reflect masterful craftsmanship. Created by Italian weaver Benedetto da Rovezzano, it dates to the 16th century.

Courtesy: The Met, New York City.

View this art in full color and resolution at RickWalker.com/9steps

STEP

3

PICK A MASTER OR ONE WILL BE THRUST UPON YOU.

What masters you defines you.

THE SET-UP: I MET REMBRANDT AND ARISTOTLE AT THE MET

Whatever masters you will define you.

In 2023, shortly after Christmas, I stood before the mystical Dutchman Rembrandt van Rijn at The Met. Shannon and the girls were already in the next gallery hall for a fashion display, while I lingered. The Met is that beloved museum nestled in New York City's Central Park; a refuge in the world's capital city.

Passing through a half-dozen lesser European galleries, I entered Rembrandt's judgment hall to stand alone with Aristotle, Homer, and Alexander. These obvious masters were on display, yet ignored. It felt like a holy place. I suspect I sinned when I shook away the inclination that the proper thing to do was to kneel. In this chapter, Alexander will teach us a little about kneeling when alone.

Rembrandt's 1653 painting, *Aristotle with a Bust of Homer*, was in front of me: hung up by nails while eternally enthroned. Only I, alone in the crowded city, worshiped with my attention. Giving your only attention is a sacrifice of everything else to one higher aim.

I wondered: could a painting of mentors arbitrage greater meaning out of the canvas and into life? I could have touched Rembrandt's Aristotle. His hat, once fully near-black, stroked with a shade of the light under his brim. I could feel the layers dimensionally with my eyes. Those mounds of oiled paints entombed by the oxidized varnish darkening the work, as it cries out for purification to restore its once-known glorious colors. If that evil varnish is removed as if it were a cataract, it would radiate the sun's light once more. The cloudy varnish reminded me of my foggy prideful mind during the campaign, waiting to be purified again.

> *"If I have seen further than others, it is by standing upon the shoulders of giants."*
> — ISAAC NEWTON

And I swear I could smell the sweat dripping down Aristotle's arm. That most intuitive man ever felt the Sculptor's flaking clay of Homer's bust as it sat on a wooden table.

Immortal Aristotle, dying in BC 322, pomply stands as he meditates on meaning and glory. Homer's bust is there who is likely the most excellent double-dimensioned author, whose literary immortality and human psychology conquered man's imagination centuries prior. *The Iliad* and *Odyssey* were Homer's works that reformulated not only minds but also the statecraft of Indian, Asian, Greek, Hebrew, and Roman kingdoms centuries after he died—his impact ripples.

The vanquished vanish while the victors rewrite history.

Courtesy: The Met, New York City.

View this art in full color and resolution at RickWalker.com/9steps

I saw the Aristotelian gold finery ornamenting the philosopher's clothing, portraying his most extraordinary student, Alexander the Great. Rembrandt's work presented three intertwined glories: Aristotle's philosophy, Homer's psychology, and Alexander's power.

Alexander,
    Wielding the story of Homer,
    Conquering the hearts of his men,
    Slaying all powers in his wake.

Homer,
    Calling forth epics out of the future,
    Overcoming the imaginations of little children,
    Molding philosophical ideology through timeless psychological insight.

Aristotle,
    Political philosopher who raised The Greatness of Alexander,
    Summoning imaginative minds to make strategic reason,
    Forming wholeness from Platonic formulation.

Each man builds on the other, regardless of his order in time. So each step in this book builds on the others.

The victors write and rewrite history—and they call forth more from you and me.

And none was greater than he to whom Alexander the Great, the greatest victor, would bend the knee. For as time bends when near the sun's weightiness, so too the proper master shapes the worthy student.

Alexander the Great was about to be remade by his new master. And you and I are a lot like Alexander.

Each of us desires a master and will take any lower substitute the moment we get free. We yearn to be slaves to shirk our responsibility and guilt.

In the previous chapter, we saw Alexander as the anti-role model—the example to avoid because of his lies, pride, and discontentment. However, I believe anyone can be redeemed.

> "Man, so long as he remains free, has no more constant and agonizing anxiety than find as quickly as possible someone to worship."
>
> — FYODOR DOSTOEVSKY

This chapter will look at the redemption of Alexander the Great through a story I suspect you have never heard before.

And it is shocking how far a story can take a man.

How deeply a bent knee to a master can remake one.

Reflect on your ideal life and imagine the questions you will need to answer to get there:

- "How can I grow as fast as possible with the least embarrassment?
- How can I simplify my work and process?
- How can I correct the failures of my past so they don't matter as much?
- How will I notice opportunities and take them on without fear?"

When you are alone, visualize your future life and relationships. Perhaps you can make a wish or two there.

THE PROBLEM: MEN NEED MASTERS

Let's be honest. Why are we all afraid to be mastered? Isn't the prudent thing to entrust what we have to someone trustworthy and who has more competency than ourselves? Instead of being logical, we are possessive, controlling, and self-serving about accepting a master and becoming a student. We prefer ideas we think we invented.

I want to understand how we can grow out of this neediness to control our finances, relationships, philosophies, and futures. Why do we try to hold on so tightly to these things?

Standing there in The Met, it became apparent that I needed to let go, trust someone, and be mastered by someone trustworthy and more competent than myself.

And isn't that what a master is—a proven competent truth-teller?

In Step 2, we discussed the importance of looking back so we could aim higher. Recall that the majority of the world's wisdom is contained in the past. And that's only logical: more time has passed before us than our present can contain.

So we need to decide not only what to be mastered by—like a great love or a worthy enemy—but also, in the end, who we shall receive mastery from.

Mastery only comes from masters.

> **TOOL: DEVELOP A MISSION**
>
> Your master mission is like a tremendous mastering vow that cascades all the lower promises of your life into order. If you don't know what you want yet, then begin with Step 1 and choose a problem to solve first. Your problem will lead you to your mission.
>
> If you know why you exist (YOUR MISSION), you will begin to see what you should value
> (YOUR VALUES) and who you can become (YOUR VISION).
>
> Download this tool for free at **RICKWALKER.COM/9STEPS**

PARADOX: HOW ALEXANDER THE GREAT BECAME JEWISH

In New York City, back at the hotel that evening, I ran down to the lobby champagne bar for some fizzy lime water. It was a few days after Christmas, and we had taken the girls to Manhattan for a Home Alone 2–themed holiday—an entirely unreasonable splurge.

Sitting at that table against the wall overlooking a little drive just off Central Park, pen and paper in hand, I wanted to know what made the walls of history stand. To arbitrage convergence and mastery, I knew I had to look back, looking through history's books for the arbitrage opportunity to gather more. For where grandeur and power reside, you must acquiesce like a student or be destroyed by what you ignore.

And the most disproportionate value is often hidden in what you ignore.

And it was a sheer mistake that I stumbled upon this—I was already sick of reading the ancient Jews but found a quote that led me down a rabbit hole to William Whiston. Desiring to get back around the Western modes, the Eastern dragged me back into their stories. I first found Whiston that winter evening on my phone. Half an hour into the limed fizz, it was time for a flat white with a single Splenda. The city never sleeps, and neither would I.

Below, I quote—three levels deep—from the 18th-century expert, William Whiston.* Taken from the words of the ancient Roman-Jewish historian Flavius Josephus, born in AD 37 in Jerusalem:

---

* William Whiston, *Of the Thundering Legion* (London: AD 1726. Pages 47–63), with some adaptations

Now Alexander, when he had taken Gaza, made haste to go up to Jerusalem. And Jaddus, the High Priest, when he heard that, was in an Agony, and under Terror; as not knowing how he should meet the Macedonians, since the King was displeased at high foregoing Disobedience. He therefore ordained, that the People should make Supplications, and should join with him in offering Sacrifice to God; whom he sought to protect that Nation; and to deliver them from the Perils that were coming upon them.

If you need a revelation, make a sacrifice. Sacrifice proceeds your revelation.

If you need a revelation, make a sacrifice.

Whereupon Jaddus was warned him in a Dream, which came upon him after he had offered sacrifice, that "He should take Courage, and adorn the City, and open the Gates; That the Rest should appear in white Garments; but that He and the Priests should meet the King in the Habits proper to their Order, without the Dread of any ill Consequences; which the Providence of God would prevent."

Upon which, when he arose from Sleep, he greatly rejoiced, and declared to all, the Warning he had received from God. According to which Warning, in his Dream, he acted entirely: And so waited for the Coming of the King...

Revelation and pain permit your joy. Only a sacrifice gives you true joy. And love is always a sacrifice.

Love is always a sacrifice.

Alexander, when he saw the Multitude at a Distance, in white Garments; while the Priests stood clothed with fine Linnen; and the High Priest in Purple and scarlet Clothing, with his Miter on his Head, having the golden Plate, whereon the name of GOD was engraved; **he approached by himself, and adored that Name, and first saluted the High Priest...**

To "salute" can often mean bowing, prostrating on the ground, or kneeling. Joy pursues wonder. More than mere happiness, proper joy gives you the energy to adventure broadly and deeply.

> *Proper joy offers you an exploration.*

Parmenio (Parmenion) alone went up to Alexander, and asked him, How it came to pass, that when all others adored him, he should adore the High Priest of the Jews? To whom Alexander the Great replied:

*"I did not adore him, but That God who has honoured him with his High Priesthood. For I saw this very Person, in a Dream, in this very Habit, when I was in Dio of Macedonia: Who, when I was considering with myself how I might obtain the Dominion of Asia, exhorted me to make no Delay, but **boldly to pass over the Sea thither**; for that he would conduct my Army, and would give me the Dominion over the Persians. Whence it is, that having seen no other in that Habit, and now seeing this Person in it; and remembering that Vision and Exhortation which I had in my Dream, **I believe that I bring this Army under the Divine Conduct**, and shall therewith conquer Darius, and destroy the Power of the Persians: **And that all Things will succeed according to what is in my own Mind."***

Wonder prosecutes boldness. You could be bold if you stopped looking down and brought your resources under a higher master.

…And when he went up into the Temple, he offered Sacrifice to God, according to the High Priest's Direction; and magnificently treated both the High Priest and the Priests.

Boldness proclaims Truth. You will find truth if you seek it boldly.

And when the Book of Daniel was shewed (shown) to him, wherein David declared that one of the Greeks should destroy the empire of the Persians, he supposed that himself was the Person intended: And as he was then glad…

Like The Met, the Jews placed that beloved Temple of Israel inside the walled refuge of Jerusalem, the capital city of the religious world of three dominant religions. Like a bullseye, this high place remains the center of all the centers of the world's meaning. And both have always attracted the most incredible men.

But imagine the faith of the High Priest, who, upon the approach of the most dominant military force ever, opened the gates; and removed their primary protection. Ludicrous.

The fortified city was protected by the walls, which were symbolic of its Protector. But that would confuse matters and world history. That which can be destroyed is less real.

Those physical gates could be opened and walls pulled down, so they were less real because they could be destroyed.

No, the fortified city had a Protector, who was symbolized by their walled protection. The physical represented the divine which cannot be destroyed. And what cannot ever be destroyed is more real than real.

> *That which can be destroyed*
> *is less real.*

I call attention to that same little nation, the Jews, without a home. For a thousand years earlier, as unarmed slaves starving in the desert, they defeated the then-greatest Egyptian military in the Red Sea. Without a scratch. Victory by a whetted wall.

Walls damned.
Weapons unneeded.
Weakness flipped.
Do you sense paradox?

Origen and Eusebius also attested to this story of Alexander's sacrifice and dream fulfillment. Israel's very existence, and Alexander the Great's enduring fame, are both testimonies that this is true. There would be no Israel if it were not.

Therefore, could it be possible that your survival to this point—through all the seeds of your pains, unanswered questions, and doubts—is evidence that you are still meant to taste the sweet fruit of them all?

A wall of the most real protection surrounds you when you live in purity and truthfulness.

- When you tell the entire truth, you are free.
- When you are free, you are available.
- When you are available, you are open to whatever joys—or pains—may come.
- For the truth makes you free. And freedom is the ultimate opportunity.

Freedom is the ultimate opportunity.

You and I continue to be like Alexander because we have the opportunity to respond as he did. That is why I stood alone in the crowd with Rembrandt's work. His work of art parallels Alexander's work of commanding an army. They both had to be mastered and to bow themselves to the highest form of what could be possible. Both Rembrandt and Alexander were students during the height of their glory. Both worshiped—the artist and the warrior. Because proper work is worship.

Work is meant to be worship.

Work should be an overflow of your purpose. If you don't worship while you work, you cannot work properly because your heart isn't in it. It's false work.

For the Jewish High Priest, his work was to obey—not mainly to open the gates and wear the vestments. It was to meet Alexander the Great without dread. Without the High Priest meeting him up close, Alexander's dream would never have been fulfilled either, and Jerusalem would certainly have been destroyed that day.

Alexander prays alone and is told that he shall see:
that man
in those robes
with that Name.

You cannot see him whom you never face. You can never expect the revelation of him to whom you never prayed. Man's greatest need is to sit quietly in a room alone. And there to face his greatest fear. You and I, like Alexander, are that man and that is our greatest need.

Praying, obeying, and bowing strip away fear.

> *Man's greatest need is to sit quietly in a room alone. And there to face his greatest fear.*

Even Alexander feared how he would conquer his enemies before he found his faith. And his finding and kneeling brought about his boldness.

> "*I believe that I bring this Army under the Divine Conduct, and shall therewith conquer Darius, and destroy the Power of the Persians: And that all Things will succeed according to what is in my own Mind.*"

To subrogate your most valued resource to the higher, remains the standard for your right sacrifice, as it was for Alexander's kneeling to the High Priest. He also submits his Army to the Divine, like a sacrifice itself.

> "Not failure, but low aim, is the crime."
> BRUCE LEE,
> *Striking Thoughts*

For the sacrifice Alexander made that day was not the offering under the direction of the High Priest. The true sacrifice was his power and identity.

Alexander, the man commonly known to read Aristotle's excerpts from the Iliad before going to sleep, had aspirations of the Homerian god-man Achilles, and kings and glory proceeding his dreaming. He looked back to the books and stories of old wiser men, as we discussed in Step 2—to aim higher you must look back. He did it in solitude.

But do not forget, while he was alone, Alexander prayed. Praying to one known—yet unnamed and unseen, or perhaps just ignored—he drifts off to awaken as a new man in his search for relevance. Perhaps bowing with wet blood still on the webbing of his fingers, and enemy frontal lobes sticking to his sandals. The right why is always the right way.

In vulnerability, Alexander the Great who dreamt of an unknown man, now kneels before the known priest, who is unguarded.

*The right why is always
the right way.*

Alexander's prophecy in his dreams, steeped in the wisdom of Homer and Aristotle, predicted the meeting of the man who would be the priest of the true God. The only way Alexander would be convinced was by the unmanufacturable. Alexander's mind's secrets must appear confirmed within the natural world. And they were. Alexander's divine visions were fulfilled only after his searching. Your prayers only invade your history after you kneel and obey. And Alexander only had his dream become reality after he prayed.

*Your prayers only invade your history
after you kneel and obey.*

The Israelites were a slippery bunch. They immediately rejected their Protector after defeating the Egyptians at the Red Sea's wall. This proves miracles do not save, they can only temporarily convince.

I saw it fitting that Alexander, the student of the greatest philosophers, was the first to act out that Plato was correct: philosophy and religion belonged together—not through intellectual reason but through imaginatively dreamed stories—and with a bent knee.

1. Painful sacrifice proceeds revelation.
2. Revelation permits joy.
3. Joy pursues wonder.
4. Wonder prosecutes boldness.
5. Boldness proclaims the truth.

You and I must listen to those higher masters as a lowly student, just like Alexander. And get alone.

AN UNDESTROYABLE KINGDOM REQUIRES AN UNDESTROYABLE KING

I was plenty satisfied to hear Alexander the Great's dream materialized, but far more remains.

The Great not only became prophet-king, in Jaddas' priestly hands, but he nearly met the prophet and king.

> And when the Book of Daniel was shewed him, wherein David declared that one of the Greeks should destroy the empire of the Persians, he (Alexander) supposed that himself was the Person intended: And as he was then glad…

That passage, which Alexander, the newly minted oracle-ruler, is said to have read as himself, comes from Daniel's seventh and eighth chapters in the Jewish scriptures. It has to do with kings and kingdoms clashing. Kings called great and who had thrones and crowns.

But, sitting there over my second flat white, I realized that for Alexander to read the first passage (Daniel 7:6) and the second portion about himself (Daniel 8:3-22), he had to read through Daniel 7:9 and 7:13-14. So the Jewish High Priest read the Hebrew text to this Greek king, and I suspect Alexander was suspicious.

Because this is what Alexander heard three centuries before Christ. The outcome of all the kings, like Alexander, from the words of Daniel:

> I beheld 'til the thrones were cast down, and the Ancient of Days (who is God the Father) did sit, whose garment was white as snow…
>
> I saw in the night visions, and, behold, one like the Son of Man (who is Christ) came with the clouds of heaven, and came to the Ancient of Days, and they brought him near before him. And there was given him dominion, and glory, and a kingdom, that all people, nations, and languages, should serve him: his dominion is **an everlasting dominion, which shall not pass away, and his kingdom that which shall not be destroyed…**

That which cannot be destroyed is more real. The Jews, whose undestroyable Protector allowed him into their destroyable gates, provided Alexander with a true revelation. Here, Alexander is introduced to an undestroyable kingdom and everlasting dominion.

This passage says the greatest kings of history, including Alexander, will cast down their thrones in worship at the feet of God, who then will hand over all dominion and glory over great kings to the Son of Man, also called Christ. Keep in mind that Alexander heard this 300 years before Christ.

A kingdom requires a king. An undestroyable kingdom means an undestroyable king. What is undestroyable is more real than anything we can see or imagine.

And I thought if Alexander was to cast off his throne, perhaps I should respond somehow. Perhaps we all should. But how?

THE LESSON:
PICK A MASTER WISELY

It's interesting that the greatest secular dominator and story-maker, Alexander the Great, bowed to the weakest nation on the planet.

I also find it odd that the leader of that weakest nation, Israel, instead of defending his people, opened the gates for the mightiest military ever known to just walk in.

Both seem like steps of faith—not logical at first glance. But both worked out.

And at some point, the lessons in great history and religion should eventually converge on us in our daily lives if they are truly real and not just facts. They must be, as we discussed in the introduction, arbitraged to be used in a place of more value than the dusty shelves next to the box of junk wrist watches. These lessons and stories which have endured millennia must invade us and cause us to act. To take a step.

Logic will only lead you so far if you want to live meaningfully. Logic must be mastered if it is to take on meaning—so must you. This is why the love of the truth powers so many scientific endeavors, and why people with imaginations command calculators to show their logic. Logic must be mastered. And it's up to you not to give in to its false promises.

You should always imagine yourself as taking the most noble action toward the most noble master.

You read above that physical protection is the least real sort of protection. Not because the physical doesn't matter. Rather, what is physical can only protect the physical. But that which is immaterial, and divine, can protect both the physical and immaterial. Why is that true?

Whatever can be destroyed—the physical—is less real than what can never be destroyed—the immaterial divine. This is why infinite love conquers a multitude of finite sins. This is why Jaddas and Alexander are no longer reigning, but He to whom they knelt as Master still sits enthroned over:

- the world's reserve currency,
- the measurement of dates,
- every 3-chorded pronouncement of Bach,
- all great classical artwork, and
- the master source of all the great literature of the English and Romantic languages.

So, if you are going to pick a master, you will want to aim high and choose like Alexander the Great also chose. His kneeling and sacrifice were to the immaterial God, not to the material needs of his military for more resources. His decision to bow and sacrifice was neither logical nor practical. But it was right. Because this finite man submitted to be mastered by a King whose kingdom could not be destroyed. And in reality, a King who would not step foot on earth for another 300 years.

And perhaps, his kneeling brought about his glory. Perhaps, your future will be more glorious because you knelt as well. Your chief error is standing when you should kneel, and kneeling when you should take a stand.

Your chief error is standing when you should kneel, and kneeling when you should take a stand.

There's a time to kneel just as there's a time to kill.

Likewise, the Jewish High Priest did not protect the physical resources and lives of his people because the higher divine call was to obey.

Truthful life and love cannot arrive except after your sacrifice, as it did not for Alexander until he entered Jerusalem. Obeying God's command means sacrificing a fake safe life for a true real life. And perhaps to the promise of a life you've only once dreamt of. And cannot explain.

Truthful life and love cannot come except by your sacrifice.

So, both King Alexander and High Priest Jaddas performed their work correctly. They submitted everything they had—their military forces and their safety—to obey their Lord.

Two chapters with inverting themes which share the same goal. Two students with the same Master who answer their opposing prayers with the same act.

And for it, they both received life, protection, and glory.

And Alexander's glory was cast backward in time to Homer and Aristotle—but also forward in time to Rembrandt because masters conquer time if we pay attention. And for some reason, they prefer to work through their students like you and me. Students mirror their masters.

And here is the fulfillment of Alexander's redemption, from the deceiver in the last chapter to the role model in this chapter. Redemptions are beautiful.

As I left New York City with my family to return home, all I could think about was what lessons might there be for me in that painting by Rembrandt.

LIFE STRATEGY:
BE MASTERED

Only a master can offer you mastery.

I've always been an early riser. I've lived in the tension of knowing that proper rest is necessary for proper health. I also felt that I needed to conquer myself and become more disciplined overall.

One of my most successful friends, who ran a much larger company than mine, told me he woke up at 4:00 AM each morning. Now for someone like me, who typically woke at 5:00 AM, hearing this was a gut punch. I thought I was already winning the morning but I was rising early, already behind.

The best masters always rise first.

My friend was already better looking than me, had more money, was way smarter, and had a better gene pool than I. I had to catch up somehow. The only resource I could use to compete was to outwork him. So, I decided to begin waking up earlier than him and investing that time in the most strategically important work I could.

> **TOOL: THE 4-POINT ACTION LOOP**
>
> Bad habits and good habits both need interruption. As you begin identifying the critical changes you need to make—your key strategies—you can use this as a tool.
>
> Download this tool for free at **RICKWALKER.COM/9STEPS**

So, I used The 4-Point Action Loop, with its roots in psychology, to try to take back the competitive advantage from the countless winners who I was sure were out there in my industry and yours:

1. I began to inch back my wake-up time by 15 minutes until it was unbearable. So, 5:00 AM became 4:45 AM the first week. And after several iterations of that, I came to 3:30 AM as the optimal wake-up time if I could get to bed by 10:00 PM. 3:15 AM was a little too early.
2. But to make that work, I had to get off all devices well before I went to bed. So I found removing my charger from my bedroom and putting the only charger in my closet—the next room over—provided two massive benefits: (a) After a couple of weeks, I stopped waking up at night and self-medicating with dopamine. So I slept straight through the night. But it also (b) triggered the next critical step in my action loop.
3. Since my phone's alarm was no longer next to my bedside, I had to walk 20 feet into my closet at 3:30 AM to turn it off. And since I didn't use a snooze feature, I turned the alarm off once.
4. As I was standing in my closet at 3:30 AM, and my motion-triggered light was on, I figured I might as well throw some clothes on.
5. Sixty seconds later and standing there dressed in a fully lit room, I went ahead and got ready for the day. I wouldn't be able to go back to sleep even if I wanted to—and I could use a good latte. Do you see how habits build on one another?
6. Once fully dressed, I got into my truck and drove 20 minutes to my office since that's the only place to get a good latte now that it's about 4:10 AM.
7. I couldn't turn on any electronics until I had read, and I enjoyed reading most with that latte in hand.
8. So after making my latte, I would sit on my favorite couch to begin

reading whatever I want. As long as it's over a thousand years old. Remember Step 2: to look up, you must look back.
9. After an hour and that first latte, I allowed myself to choose to do anything I wished for the next couple of hours as long as I was not looking at a screen. So I began to prefer silence, old books, and a paper planning notebook.

In this action loop, or habit loop as author James Clear calls it, I replaced my old masters—sleep and screens—with a new master who is higher and better. That newer master—the one contained in the ancient books and silence—brings me peace, power, and truth—not because I sought those things, but because I was willing to be mastered by them.

And being alone, you sometimes offer up a prayer. And sometimes prayers find themselves answered in real life. But they look less like lotteries, fame, and job promotions, and more like restoration of loves, healing of tumors, and moments of wisdom.

YOUR NEXT MOVES

As water only flows downhill, so too mastery only flows down to you if you are below looking up for it. Your humility plays a role, and so too does your position. Order matters. And you must be below to look up. That was Step 2.

As you begin to seek a master, look around you. See how the world, nations, literature, and the arts function. Look at the basis of laws and religions. Notice overlapping meta ideas and concepts. For all laws and religions only steal their truths. Truth is always the way.

And from Truth, look for competence and trustworthiness. Again, I recommend you look at least a thousand years back. Because time will purge most, but not all, the lesser ideas. And from those ancient ideals, you will look for the men who did the most benefit to the world. Who worked hardest to end the slave trade, tried to assassinate Hitler, promoted freedoms, and fed the poorest? And from that list, see if there is a common source.

These two tasks—the searches for underlying truth and world-shattering competence—are how you begin to uncover the ideal master. This search is the student's admission into the correct classroom, and it is how you become a student living a meaning-filled life of growth.

You need to be mastered by someone greater than yourself. Consider how you can use the 4-Point Action Loop to create one new habit as you consider the following:

- Replace that worst thing you do with an activity that is the next best thing you can imagine for 30 days.
- Replace one low-minded activity with one high-aimed move in the next hour.
- Replace an hour of your daily distracted time with a half-hour of alone time first thing each morning.

Alexander was mentored by Aristotle. They were both mentored by Homer's books and fashioned their strategies around his epic stories. You and I are like Alexander: we need a higher mentor who offers us the possibility of living out an epic higher story.

But first, we will move one level deeper to analyze the beginning of Homer's Trojan epic which Alexander kept in his coat pocket to read at night after his prayers. The next chapter pair—Step 4 and Step 5—will concern the circumstances of our lives in the same order this first pair came: a seascape story of defeat then a seascape story of defeat's inversion. The demise of defeat.

But without the seaside defeat we will describe next, there would never have been an Alexander the Great for us to model or to spite.

Be conquered by the highest master you can find. And get alone in silence.

PAIR B:
OUR EXTERNAL DECLINE AND ASCENT

"Consider the subtleness of the sea; how its most dreaded creatures glide under water, unapparent for the most part, and treacherously hidden beneath the loveliest tints of azure. Consider also the devilish brilliance and beauty of many of its most remorseless tribes, as the dainty embellished shape of many species of sharks. Consider, once more, the universal cannibalism of the sea; all whose creatures prey upon each other, carrying on eternal war since the world began."

HERMAN MELVILLE
Moby Dick

The Sacrifice of Iphigeneia by Gaetano Gandolfi Rococo is a dramatic oil painting depicting the mythological moment of Iphigeneia's near-sacrifice, blending dynamic composition, emotional intensity, and masterful chiaroscuro. The artwork embodies Gandolfi's Rococo style with classical influences, capturing human despair and divine intervention. The Metropolitan Museum of Art, New York.

Courtesy: The Met, New York City.

View this art in full color and resolution at RickWalker.com/9steps

STEP 4

TRUST REVELATION REQUIRES SACRIFICE.

*If you are unsure of your purpose,
here's how to make a proper sacrifice.*

THE FAST:
MY 7-DAY SACRIFICE

SACRIFICE BRINGS REVELATION.
As we kick off the second chapter pair, we take a look at the first of two seascapes. Like the chapters on Alexander, the second corrects the first. But the first is still true. Both myths and both historical.

My right eye cannot open all the way. It's more noticeable some mornings, but essentially I'm not runway-ready anymore. The 3-inch scar down my neck doesn't help.

And I suspect since you and I are so much alike deep down, you also have these scars, ticks, and imperfections that you think everyone notices but they rarely do. We think about the surface level, the superficial, instead of the deeper experiences and what caused them. And why they are there in the first place. I sure do.

It was August 2013. Now living in Houston, I hurried between cities wearing my tackiest patterned suits and sockless loafers. I had grand conversations while dismissing everyone else around me as somehow less than I was, prudes or friendless freaks. I silently judged everyone and squashed the part of me that understood this was my raging ego, propelling me into a bad person.

Something needed to change. I couldn't shake the feeling that my efforts to be a good man by outworking everyone and building a prosperous future for my family had somehow led me to drift off course from who I could become. Success is always relative.

I would start with my mind, through my body. My friend Chuck did these brutal 40-day fasts annually. With his encouragement, I began with a 7-day fast. A sacrifice of what I desired to obtain the clarity I needed. Only Houston's finest tap blend and non-dairy juices. I committed to the process, as I stuck to many other systemized plans throughout my life. And I felt terrific for two days. I was starving by the third. By day four, my toxin-evicting leg cramps grew so challenging to manage that I spent that day at a park, walking circles around the ponds. I'd walk until I got tired and sit on the hard bench. On the fifth day, I brought Plato's Republic to keep me busy. When I rested on the bench, I started reading deeply from the wisdom of the ancients.

On the sixth day, between reading and walking, I felt a sense of despair and fear drift up from my gut, chest, or heart. I couldn't lock down where it came from or what it was, but it came with a sense of tunnel vision and confusion. I sat on the bench, gripped the wooden seat with both hands and suddenly felt uncertain about everything around me.

I knew it wasn't an external terror. I nervously sensed the scent of myself on this emotion—my organs, my intellect, my desires, and perhaps, my spirit. But if anything was askew in any of those, it would prove to be unsolvable alone. I sat there panicked with an unknown problem I could not take on by myself. For once, this unknown unknown had to wait in tension for an answer.

When I slowly shook free of the sensations, I sent a note to my assistant, asking her to find the top executive health exam possible. I was afraid for some reason, but I didn't know why.

My fast brought immense clarity. My mind could hear my body. My body could feel the authority of the fasting, which thwarted my years of self-control over my entire schedule. I wasn't overweight, but meals were always the building blocks of my calendar. And if my calendar, then my time. My time, my life. The fast took meals off the schedule and threw me out of my false sense of control over time.

Perhaps I was so rattled because I always felt time was the lone resource.

After booking it, I decided to find out what an executive exam was. Was this a blood work and physical only, or would the doctor invade?

Do you ever have those close calls when driving that make you ruminate on what could have happened? Do you think about your mortality often? You see if you have not done either recently, I can promise you your mortality will begin to guide your morality. It did for me. And you and I aren't that different once you peel away some experiences and undeserved wins. Your story may be a little like my story.

THE EXAM

After checking into that massive exam room at Methodist in Houston, I stripped out of that suit to wear workout gear. My sneakers hit the track of the treadmill under the doctor's watchful eye. Steps became strides, and strides turned into a sprint.

Following that were the eight vials of blood and the scans of my heart, larger arteries, and lungs in rapid-fire succession. No issues so far.

Following the scans, I returned to the original room and changed into an exam gown. Sometimes an object pre-reflects what is to come.

The nearly eighty-year-old doctor with icy hands but warm words entered the room for the personal touch. Those hands had examined celebrities, presidents, and executives for years.

He conducted a full-body examination of all my skin, abdomen, feet, genitals, and hairline. He found some moles, which he asked me to follow up with my dermatologist about, but they were nothing. Washing his hands, he made small talk to ease the uneasiness in the air, and I figured he was done, so I thought about my flight to D.C. later that day.

But after drying and sanitizing, the doctor felt my head, examined my mouth, and ran his fingers down my neck. Fingertips running and pressing to test the tautness eyes cannot see. Across my scalp, from hairline to hairline, ear to ear. Beginning below my mouth, he methodically worked his icy digits in waves as a diligent mother would ice a cake sure to cover every inch. Down, pressing in on the left side under my jaw and over to my left ear. Down the left side sweeping down to my collarbone. Then over to my jaw under the right side. Midway through his movement over my right neck, his in-and-out pressure became more circular and firm.

"Hmm."

My eyes, which had been closed out of the awkwardness of the day's prior events, opened. His closed in concentration.

"How long have you had this nodule in your neck? Can you feel this right here?"

"I don't know."

"We need to get a better look at this. Today."

"I have to catch a flight to D.C. in three hours."

"I don't think you want to fly."

The positive for the day, and with every healthy younger male, was that his fingers stayed on the outside of my body. The negative was that the exam turned out differently than I had hoped. He ordered an M.R.I. and a P.E.T. immediately.

The doctor found the abnormality my intuition knew I had.

What the doctor felt, and the imaging found, was a spherical mass at the joining of my interior and exterior carotid arteries between my throat and my right ear. One of the scans, which I still have on DVD, showed a three-dimensional tumor that had parasitically grown to become part of the walls where the interior and exterior arteries met. Arteries are only walls, so that sounded like an issue to me.

A DVD sneaks a threat into my life once again.

I recalled noting for years, even in elementary school, that my fingers felt a bulge each time I rubbed my pulsing neck. The irony was that my fingertips could feel my own demise each time I sought to feel for my heartbeat. Death, like evil, had always been waiting for me in the place I always sensed it growing but never wanted to acknowledge. We all avoid it.

Figuratively, I needed a shaman to dislodge the demonic presence that unknowingly held me at ransom my entire life. All three: my pride, my sin, and my tumor lurked beneath the surface as a triple threat.

I became aware I was a mortal man in a moment. But at least a man who knows he can die can kill pride easier than someone who suspects he is invincible.

A man who knows he can die can kill pride easier than someone who suspects he is invincible.

As I sat in that parking garage in silence, I was trying to decide if I was going to catch my pending flight to D.C. or get the scans as the doctor advised; I breathed in and out in bewilderment at what to do next.

Should I call Shannon to tell her over the phone? Is it best to travel and wait until I get home to tell her in person? Should I even tell her?

I decided to do the weak thing. I boarded that flight, deciding to tell her when I returned home in a few days. But aboard, I couldn't help but wonder why the doctor told me not to fly today. Would this tumor pop under the pressure of the cabin? Could it grow in the altitude to constrict my breathing or blood? I didn't ask—I just disobeyed.

All rebels disobey authority.

You need to think about your future and ask,

- "What am I avoiding that I know I must do?
- What moments of clarity and wise advice have I brushed aside to choose comfort instead?
- Why do I always eventually get misery when I choose comfort?
- Why do I buck against authority and prefer instead to invent my logic?"

I WAS STABBED IN THE NECK

The carotid is one of the two main routes to feed blood to the face and brain. But since the walls of the interior carotid and the exterior carotid met, that Y-shaped meeting point was also the tumor itself. So came the complexity.

Sometimes, your sacrifice is the enemy that appears to be keeping you alive. Often you can't pick your sacrifice. You and I are still like Alexander in that regard.

The surgeon pulled a blue Bic from his white lab coat pocket protector. Sketching a diagram on a torn-off piece of exam table rolled paper, he showed me how he would dissect the artery above and below the tumor, remove it, and then attempt to patch and run a new bypass to reconnect my brain to my heart. And, of course, time was of the essence. My brain and face both needed that blood, as much as I needed my head.

After a round of specialist appointments, a major surgical procedure was scheduled a few days later. They told me to plan on potentially spending two weeks in the ICU. Understanding the risks and sporting shorts and a tear-soaked shirt, I wrote goodbye letters to my three little girls, who were each under six. I told them who I wanted to walk them down the aisle. Who to trust. How to help their Mom. The type of man I would approve of them marrying.

I also had to make some adjustments for the businesses. So, I created redundancies wherever I could find, such as adding additional admins to the bank accounts and making lists for Shannon—lists of entities, people, employees, passwords, investments, and life insurance policies. Thankfully, we had a great team at work, and I knew they would be fine for a year or so.

I didn't sleep much, either. Instead of trying to go back to sleep when I woke up in the middle of the night, I jumped on my computer to make just one more plan or safeguard for Shannon. My biggest fear was that she'd get frustrated in dealing with the employees and just shut the companies down. So, I spent time showing her which companies made money and which she could expect to lose because they were long-term. Like a laddered investment, I had founded a variety of long-term and short-term companies with different profitability maturities.

When I left for the hospital, I was incredibly concerned that my goodbyes to my daughters could be final. Complications matter. I fought back tears until I got into the car, but only then I broke down. Hands covering my face, tears pouring down my cheeks and over my tumor.

In the silence of that car ride with Shannon driving:

- I thought about the future we may never get.
- I thought about her next husband: the guy who would benefit from all my hard work like the lazy son-of-a-bitch I knew he'd be.
- I considered the possibility of unknown side effects like paralysis of my body or my mind.

The fear set in for a wake-up.

We checked into the Marriott across the street from the hospital because I had a 4:00 AM call time the following day. After grabbing some Salata with my folks, we prayed for the surgeon's skill and went to bed.

Lying in that damp bed—where a thousand others have helplessly wept for their loved ones in the hospitals all around—all I wanted was to hold Shannon's hand. To be back in the house hugging my little girls. I was 34 years old and, at that moment, I finally felt like a worthy father. Moments are all we have.

For I finally understood that clinging the hand of my love in the throes of dark uncertainty is the best hope anyone can hold when life is on the line. And life is always on the line.

Walking across the over-road sky bridge connecting the hotel and the hospital, I gave Shannon everything in my pockets, and the 1990s Omega Speedmaster my Dad gave me for graduation slipped off my wrist. The white face, with gold bezel, was still fitted with the brown crocodile band it shipped with. Should I warn her it runs a little fast if you don't demagnetize it monthly? It felt more like checking in for prison.

Once we checked in, on schedule, they sent me back to change. In the pre-op, I made two requests of the nurses and the anesthesiologist. The first was they promised they would remove the catheter BEFORE I woke up. And the second was that I could see Dr. Smith with my eyes before they knocked me out. I feared Dr. Smith, the OBGYN, would show up first instead of Dr. Smith, the Cardiologist.

Lying there behind those cold curtains alone, I thought of the dozens of older men with fuller lives who likely already died in this same drab gown—with plenty of stains—I was now wearing. That gown was cursed.

The irony of my only two requests was that for me to see Dr. Smith and remain on schedule, they'd have to cath me before I went to sleep. And I might feel it. To feel it going in would be way worse than coming out. No thanks. As the lighter anesthesia went in so that they could prepare for a heavy line, the right Dr. Smith came in just as I passed out.

And once passed out, they installed a PICC line entering my neck and down into my heart. I entered a deeper sleep than I had ever known.

Here lies a poor bastard with a rich ego, humbly praying for pity for the first time.

THE REVELATION:
THE ART OF A MIRACLE

The surgeon's report was brief: As the chilly scalpel stabbed then sliced open my warm neck, then stopped, the surgeon's light—powered by solar panels from the sun's lighted heat a million miles away—flashed off the surgical blade and into my body.

To light up the unexpected.

The tumor of destruction had not only disconnected from the artery (which the 3D DVD showed it was part of), but it also simultaneously self-healed. Yes, the multiple walls of the Y-shaped artery's intersection self-healed instantly, so I didn't bleed out and die from the first miracle.

Order matters. True simultaneity of two consecutive miracles is doubly impossible. But the tumor had also doubled in size over the two weeks since it was diagnosed, making its discovery after waiting dormantly for decades, incalculably timely. I had lived a thousand weeks with it, but the only two that counted were these.

The tumor could have taken me at any of those moments. Yet, in the sole moment among the millions, the tripled miracle occurred: detachment, self-healing, and timing at the same point in time.

Probabilities matter. This tripled impossibility multiplied together in an improbable moment.

That skilled cardiovascular surgeon reached into my neck with his gloved thumb and pointer finger to retrieve the tumor intact, emerging the size of a great egg.

> *I imagine the tumor being pulled from the dark where it had been thriving off my blood. It takes its first breath in that light which ends its plan to thrive hidden in my darkness. Like a spy, planted on the inside since my birth, he was waiting for this specific time to bloom fully into Death. Now the red fleshy ball is angry he was discovered by his opponent in the most improbable of fashions—a once-in-a-lifetime fast and prayer. He squirms, trying to reenter, but instead falls to the freshly waxed floor in the surgical room.*

The terminal threat inside my body not only resolved but simultaneously repaired multiple locations in an instant before my body was opened. Order matters—even for tripled miracles. It happened inside of me, which makes it personal because I know there was no tampering with the evidence. It was my eyes that witnessed the multiple interactive images taken from multiple hospitals—my fingers, which felt through my young skin—my hands working the computer to inspect at every angle. The blue pen sketch on hand-torn paper diagramming his planned work—a man who had done hundreds of these surgeries before.

The impossible miracle now stands irrevocably imminent inside me. The incredible event did not just take place inside me; it was my very body and veins that participated in the incredible assault on the causal claims of the medical sciences and logic. Miracles are the divine breaking into nature. At just the right moment.

For me, like Israel's very existence in the last chapter, the fact that I'm alive is a testament that a single miracle happened at one point in history. And I suspect if you will look back closely enough—like into that car wreck your mother was in before she had you—you too will find that sole miracle evidenced by your very living. Don't miss the magic of the unmanufacturable.

A WRAPPED MOMENT

I recall that Christmas. Waking up—it is the best day ever. Shannon, before walking over to be with the kids opening their gifts, first hands me something special. This is a wrapped moment. And ripping the paper across the face of the glassy plane, I realized what she had done. She saved it. She had that doctor's blue pen drawing on the torn-off exam paper, that symbol of the unexpected miracle, mounted in a frame. I was shocked by her forethought and immediately knew where it should go. I needed to see this every single day before I did anything. I took the drill and a couple of Phillip's heads from yet-to-be-painted garage cabinets and immediately hung it in my closet to see morning and evening.

Whatever happens once can happen again.

This is a literal, not just figurative, testimony to the art of a miracle. For the framed art of the surgeon was itself made untrue by a single miraculous act inside me. His thumb which held the blue pen as it diagrammed an ordinary plan was redeemed as it pulled death's defeat out of my neck in an extraordinary act. That was a revelation.

Whatever happens once
can happen again.

If a miracle can happen to this poor prude, it can happen to anyone. If you fight, you have to be prepared to take a hit. If you are cut open, you have to be prepared to be dug out. And it's often the threat of the cuts and hits that lure you out of fighting and back into safety.

I didn't want to be cut open to have that tumor removed. I didn't like the risk to my mind and face from the surgery. I didn't pick that sort of sacrifice. But had I not listened to that small voice during my 7-day fast and solitude, not only would I not have received that miracle and revelation, I may not have even lived to know I missed it.

Your rejection of solitude and risk means the rejection of miracles and real life. Let me show you a better way.

THE SET-UP:
AGAMEMNON

Stories make men. Great stories make greater men.

As we learned from Alexander the Great's stories, revelation and redemption will necessarily include solitude with a sacrifice of pride, safety, or life. He learned this from Homer, who may be one of the greatest makers of great men.

And now allow me to set up the first story in the pair: the defeat at sea.

> *A candlelit banquet hall of white shimmering granite hewn a thousand years prior. Pigs stew in vast spiced cauldrons. Families feast around dinner tables in new-found consummatory peace. Paris's brown solid eyes meet Helen of Troy's icy blue. Paris was the youngest son of Trojan King Priam. Helen was the prize of Spartan King Menelaus. Menalaus' most powerful brother was Agamemnon, Lord of all the Bronze Age Greeks.*
>
> *Helen stowed in the Trojan ship to slip away with Paris. And she sets the world aflame for the most extraordinary epic.*

I've found strong men are always searching for war. For a challenge. For an enemy. The Greeks here mobilize the greatest army ever seen at their port on the Aegean Sea to reach their foe. To sail their thousand-plus fleet westward. Blue sky. Golden sun. But a supernaturally darkened sea disrupts them. Howling waves crest over the ships. The warriors cannot board, for the gusts and tides are prevalent and ominous. It's a stormy seascape of Biblical proportions. The commander, Agamemnon, cannot calm the stormy seas.

Artemis, who is Diana in the Roman manifestation, is still angry at King Agamemnon's boasting of being a superior hunter to the goddess. So, he enlists his seer, Calchas, to appease the war goddess with the blood of peaceful doves. But everyone knows peaceful doves are a feast that cannot please a warrior. She desires a more proper, noble blood if they are to cross over the sea of chaos and threat.

Agamemnon made a hurried vow to lure his wife and daughter Iphigeneia to the Aulis port. He used mediators Odysseus and Diomedes to deceive and restrain his wife, Clytemnestra, to send his daughter so that she might wed the great half-god, Achilles.

Arriving in her wedding pomp, Iphigeneia ascends the hill with her father. Atop, she finds an unexpected stone table and priest where she expected to find a reception dinner table. She finds death at this granite altar where she expects to find new life—a steeled blade instead of a steel ring, death instead of that eternal circle.

> *"I have met the enemy and he is me."*
> ALEXANDER THE GREAT

But after her momentary struggle, she succumbs to willing slaughter. The innocent lamb, Iphigeneia, is given up on Artemis' granite dinner table of war to make way for the Greek crossing. (Merely traded to Artemis for a female deer in some variations, but still lost.)

Agamemnon's most loved, innocent daughter was sacrificed for what he wrongly most desired—to take back the most remarkable beauty, Helen of Troy. And leave Troy in ruins.

Like Agamemnon, we too defile our lives by giving into the unholy low things, like war and thoughtless anger, at the cost of our high and lovely treasure, like our family.

Our futures are determined by the tables of our dinners and our sacrifices.

YOUR PAST MUST BE SACRIFICED

My studies of the various ancient religious traditions revealed a universal fact: any ultimate conquest requires an ultimate sacrifice. Alexander and

Agamemnon knew that all too well. As I mentioned in the introduction, I'm hardly a Christian and not much of an Agnostic…but a little of both. But that surgery-less miracle to remove and heal my tumor at just the right time spoke a little more faith into my heart than was there before. Not a ton, but a little.

Perhaps like you, I've waffled between selfless honor and dishonest selfishness my whole life. And from this pitied position I have found myself studying a variety of Eastern and Western religions and philosophies, like a wandering boy flipping through the television channels. The options are many, but the themes are few. Sacrifice is one of those meta themes.

As you contemplate the road just ahead, you will inevitably get bogged down in the mistakes you've made and the false masters you've served. And the regrets. Just like me. Maybe these come in the form of missed opportunities and lost loves. Perhaps these look like sins of pride, jealousy, broken family relationships, sexual addiction, fear, loneliness, or witchcraft which started as an innocent game. And it's gotten hold of you in a way you subconsciously believe that a horrible past will control your future possibilities.

Your sins drive your fears. And your fears control your future. How will you break free?

You need some solitude. Perhaps a fast instead of a feast. And there to visualize your path forward as a new man instead. To be restored and redeemed. To be, and I hate to use this tainted word, forgiven by yourself. It's often your own thinking and lack of respect for yourself that tears down your own dreams before you ever take a step. Solitude and sacrifice will help.

Your enslavement by your past must itself be enslaved by your new Master. And your solitude and sacrifice of your past look a lot like kneeling to God's masterful vision for your future. And His vision becomes your revelation if you will allow it.

But first, you must choose whether to give up on your future or give up your past to Him.

TAINTED SACRIFICES

Between 1998 and 2017, I, too, made many rash vows and improper sacrifices like Agamemnon did with those peaceful doves. How did I do that? I used a good thing to cover up a selfish thing. I tried to evade the detection of my low sins with the distraction of a mediocre gift. Let me explain.

During this period, I started giving away 30-60% of my annual income to charities. But I did it expecting a return of blessing. I misused the universal truth that giving is the blessing, not receiving. I mirrored Agamemnon in thinking I was the superior hunter-god and could fool the gods with a token offering. So my sacrifices, which I assumed were accepted, were, in reality, rejected.

I was misusing a divine command: give, and it will be given to you. But the understood rule in the Christmas command is that I must give expecting not to receive back if I hope to obtain any real blessing at all. I got it all wrong.

So, instead of committing my time and money to help, I gave to charities as an investor, trusting I'd get more back from heaven. My reasons revoked my actions because I didn't realize my why matters more than my actions. My wrong why led me the wrong way and into a false future. An unholy why becomes an unholy sacrifice.

Wrong reasons
revoke right actions.

So, the purpose of giving away that filthy lucre—often anonymously—was the same as Agamemnon's seer sacrificing doves to Artemis: I was trying to give an inferior offering up to impact my eternal future.

In doing so, I, like Agamemnon at Troy, wasted a decade at the gates of relevance I wished to storm. From 2007 to 2017, a generation of my relevance and the impact of my capital vanished—business, charity, happiness, and mental clarity—because I did the right thing with the wrong expectations. I gave a good gift to a holy God for a tainted purpose.

And since you and I are basically the same, have you considered what unholy activity you justify using a fake excuse because you know you need to give it up?

Excuses are rarely reasons.

OUR RASH VOWS

Trying to keep the wrong thing, you lose everything.

But why does this happen? How could I even know this? Perhaps it's because Alexander, after praying and kneeling, gets eternal glory. After he submits his army under the leadership of Divine Conduct—his words, not mine—he conquers most of the known world. He risks, sacrifices, the most powerful military ever known and kneels before the weakest people whose gates are wide open for plunder.

And by giving away the right thing he gains more power.

Now, we all know we will be sacrificed by the hand of time. For time shall both be the hand of our executioner—and our corpse's grave-bound carriage. But why?

> *All your prior moments have been sacrificed to your present.*

In haste, we all self-curse reality by making rash vows and lowly sacrifices like Agamemnon and me. What might this look like in your life?

- A man marries based on lust. Or money.
- A man votes to guess the winner.
- A woman chooses the lesser work of an hourly job over the more significant work of motherhood whenever she does work she hates.

Marriage, voting, and working are all good but are perverted when done with the wrong motivations.

Yet sometimes even doing the wrong thing for the right reason is enough. Iphigeneia's submission to her father to save her people was a lovely why amid her father's heinous sacrifice. Nothing worth doing is easy.

Isn't it that option to choose the right attitude that makes being human complex, yet lovely? Humanity dictates optionality, but optionality requires freedom. She decided to die willingly, despite the ugliness of her father-king.

Your free will is both: your highest opportunity to sacrifice well and your worst threat of sacrificing wrong.

Because it requires pain, a proper sacrifice is difficult but beautiful. If you can overcome your desires for a risk-free and painless life, you fill the world with a drop of beauty. And beauty is as good as power. Ask Helen of Troy.

> *Beauty is as good as power.*

Contemplate what this means for you. You have the option to make rash vows like Agamemnon or make yourself a willing sacrifice like Iphigeneia. The same act. She was giving and beautiful. He was wrong and ugly.

But be warned: when your pride is at most risk, you will make your worst decisions and rashest promises to serve your lowest impulses.

However, when you find a little solitude and the right reason, you might just obtain a revelation. Imagine your best future and ask yourself,

- "Why couldn't my future be remade out of something better than my failed past?
- Why couldn't I send up a prayer of surrender as a white flag that my will is at His behest?
- How can I get brave enough to trust someone more intelligent and more competent than me?
- What could I do if I didn't care about what I did because my whys were always right?"

A BIGGER PROBLEM: MY MENTAL FOG

Sacrifices only bring a full revelation once you feel the full weight of their cost.

Unfortunately, over the first few weeks of my recovery from surgery, my mental processing slowed noticeably. I couldn't tell whether it was cloudy or delayed, but I couldn't respond to complex ideas very well. A comment here and there was problematic for me to conceptualize. My reading, limited as it was, laboursome.

The 7-day fast, a kind of false sacrifice to please my guilty self, gave me mental clarity at first, but it did the opposite in the end. But it did save my life and prove miracles.

I tried every kind of supplement, and all the diets, but nothing seemed to return my thwarted thinking to my pre-surgery strength. I did not discuss it, not even with Shannon. I feared I would have a psychological defect and be medicated as such. That, to me, was the downside that no upside could overcome.

I think everyone is a little concerned with that threat—the threat of dementia or cognitive challenge. And so we hide what we suspect until it grows untreatable. Like all lies. Like all moral tumors.

And when in the presence of individuals of world-class competency, I could no longer function at the level I wanted. The delays became stammering. I tried to fix the stammering, but that consumed my remaining mental RAM, which was now turned inward to evaluate how I was being perceived—a vicious circle.

But this playing from behind was a new me. I had squandered the gift of my mind. And I didn't feel like myself, as much of who I had become rested on my ability to communicate and to contemplate. And it persisted.

It was most noticeable when alone or in deeply contemplative conversations, which I began to avoid.

I was processing at half speed. Months turned to years...it would be shown publicly by a series of poor decisions when I ran for US Congress and needed to scale my businesses again.

And in solitude, I prayed a second time: for God to give me a drop from the ocean of His wisdom.

Drops build oceans.

SOMETHING'S GOTTA GIVE

But even in my plight—a broken marriage, declining businesses, and post-campaign embarrassment—I had enough sense to imagine even though I couldn't think very well.

What should you think about when finding a solution?

Dante says we make rash vows if we don't lay down our will on an altar of sacrifice. That seemed to harken back to the Iphigeneian sacrifice of Agamemnon. Anything worth keeping is worth sacrificing. Nothing not worth keeping is worthy of offering.

Everything worth keeping is worth sacrificing.
Nothing not worth keeping is worthy of offering.

But what if all you have left is you? And you are a little broken.

Then you must make the crawl. You must crawl, bleeding hands and knees, onto the altar table of the gods.

If Agamemnon had not surrendered his will to Artemis, the waters would have dashed the Greeks upon the rocks before landing into their future on the Trojan shores. Had his beloved child not laid down her will, she would not have been able to obey her father and king.

What do you have that you could sacrifice?

All I had left was me—broke and broken. And a stubborn will. But what would happen if I could figure out a way to give up my will?

Dante taught me to believe—not as a fact but as a hope—that once my will was surrendered, the unimaginable future would begin to manifest.

That my undying eternal will—the prideful part of it that nearly took down my family during the campaign—would die of its own volition. I relied on the evidence from Homer, Alexander, and Dante that only my will could permit itself to die.

How does it work that way? How are our wants and desires connected to the future?

Dante calls my why to be pointed somewhere. All our whys are always aimed. Remember Step 2: aim high because aiming low is the only sin. It is my why that must be first aimed.

> *The quality of the altar makes the quality of the gift.*

Like Alexander the Great, we must take a step to get a revelation. To step forward in the highest, truest, and most noble sense would be for us to direct ourselves toward the horizon of Christ who is Truth Himself. Truth, not always apparent, must be leapt at. He cannot be safely approached while we stand stunned in fear by the challenge of sacrifice. To mount any granite slab always necessitates a leap of faith. Does it surprise you that the highest altar requires the highest leap?

Only the will can lay itself down as a sacrifice eternally, forever pointing itself rightly. And it does so not because it is not wise. But because it is.

We rebels cannot be trusted. For every other sacrifice may be taken back off the altar, bringing a self-caused curse. Only the wise will, will not will itself back to itself.

But something worthy, honest, and valuable had to be given up beyond just a promise to be good and obey God. What useful and tangible thing did I have left worthy to offer as a sacrifice?

Eventually, sacrifices must move beyond the abstract and into the concrete if they are to be authentic.

SACRIFICING 90% OF MY NET WORTH

The ego must die before a man can live. And since my fast only hurt me and did not build me like I wanted, I knew something more drastic than a 7-day fast, exam, or surgery needed to be done. Did I need to cut away a more significant, more valuable growth I didn't realize was taking over my life? The one that fed my ego and provided the safety I hid beneath?

Others have said that the humble will inherit mansions. But I recalled a central theme in every great epic and religion: when I did wrong or needed a miracle, the right move was to make a sacrifice. And it had to be something to give up that I wanted badly to keep—for my survival. Because to sacrifice something insignificant is an offense to the gods.

Alexander the Great's sacrifice in Jerusalem wasn't a goat or ox because those didn't matter to him. Losing animals didn't hurt him. Instead, Alexander sacrificed his pride and his army as he put them under the Divine Conduct to see his dreams become reality. Jaddas, the High Priest, gave up the entire Jewish people when he opened the gates to see Jerusalem saved. What did a broken man like me have left? Could there be a physical something that would enable me to give away my will?

Remember, I had tried to hack the system by giving away money to good charities for selfishly wrong desires. But the hack backfired. An unworthy gift becomes a curse on the giver. It proved that my sacrifice for over a decade was an unworthy offering. So mere money would not work. But what about the source of all my money?

An unworthy gift becomes a curse on the giver.

In 2014, my Dad retired from my largest real estate company, where he was managing quality control. He thought he'd spend his retirement helping my sister and her kids in Oklahoma City and spending time with us. But my Mom still worked, so he didn't travel as much as he would have liked. They preferred to travel together. So, he slowed down. And without any hobbies, his boredom turned into fatigue. He wanted something to do. Dad needed a purpose. I needed a worthy sacrifice.

But what did he really need? I've always found hard work with a smidge of status drives purpose. A Veteran once based in Korea, he loved to travel around to military bases to visit the commissaries and canteens. Knowing that, I started sending him to conduct tours of our federal contracting business operations. That was perfect because it also involved his second favorite activity: sampling the bulgogi at Korean restaurants around Texas & Oklahoma. He enjoyed being there among other Veterans his age, then he got the opportunity to drive to the next stop. He popped in to visit my sister in Oklahoma and us in Houston regularly.

But what did I need now in 2019 to heal my broken family and other work projects after the campaign the year prior? I needed to focus on my wife and daughters. That required attention. I needed to spend a few months fixing my marriage while also looking for my next big business project. However, I knew I wasn't in the right place spiritually because selfishness came too easily. I was still entrenched in a prideful pursuit, only now shown to be a loser on national television. Either I could wait this out, or I could do what I always have done. I could take a significant action based on intuition—to prove to myself that I had sacrificed my will in an unalterable way. It would also respect the history of every primary belief system, including Jaddas, Dante, and Alexander.

But what I needed even more, as a man, was to see if I still had my mojo. How big a boy was I? Could I rebuild it all again, or was it a fluke? Was I a fluke?

And after a few months of not having an enemy, I remembered Step 1: choose one worthy enemy.

So, I did the unthinkable. I had the attorneys draw up the paperwork, and a federal government agency liaison reviewed and approved it. I sent the paperwork over to my Dad, just telling him he's back in the game. Once he signed, I lost 90% of my net worth and 100% of my largest company. Sometimes, circumstances are the best enemy to choose.

After building a life and investments primarily from a single business, I gave the business ownership away to my Dad—all of it—and resigned.

So, in 2019, I sacrificed my safety and primary career, which had paid for nearly everything, while the other companies were bleeding cash. This meant I had a negative income with almost no money on hand—less than a month's cash. Sharks tasting my blood in the business waters would likely maul me.

But no one could ever say I didn't play hard. And no one could ever say I got lucky if I could do it again from nothing.

MY IDENTITY LOST

Shockingly, my life shifted when that part of me ended. Perhaps it was the new challenge of scrappily rebuilding a business without cash and my home life teetering. My shameful public devastation from the loss of the campaign. My marriage in shambles. The source of most of my money and safety gone. Identity as a successful leader lost.

And with a broken marriage, business, and importance, I hit rock bottom. No more GQ parties, billionaire meet-ups, big board seats, exciting projects, or family vacations. It felt as if every stone I had built up had been torn down and thrown at me in my stoning as a heretic—and they were thrown by everyone I ever loved. I was a rebel who sought to outdo everyone for my own glory, then they turned on me.

Every pathetic man thinks of himself as a victim.

But I had just made a gigantic bet. A bet on my need for more pressure, not less. A bet that giving with the proper purpose was the vehicle to receiving. A bet I could again become a victor.

And I imagine some of you cocky men reading this now need more pressure, not less.

Was I my Mom's false prophecy whose predictions of success were never to happen? And worse than that—a man who turned everyone else's predictions of what potential I could or would do with my life a decade earlier into a lie? Would my concrete accomplishments forever be turned backward into potential then dissolved away into meaninglessness?

Hanging my head, I went back to work on the business. We had a ton of extra staff whose jobs could be outsourced to partners. They were great people, but just outdated positions who could be moved to subcontractors or positions reimagined for a new economy. That removed a ton of complexity in the day-to-day operations.

Keeping someone in an outdated position out of pity is falsifying their entire effort, if purpose is tied to work. You can't do it.

I think it was Peter Drucker who once quipped that the most efficient company would only have one employee. I got that. I might have thought hard about how to get there.

Moving those folks to a hybrid of outsourced services firms worked out well for the company and for them. I was able to upgrade the management team. Over the three years after, our team averaged about 100 commercial real estate transactions per year across high-rise office buildings, retail centers, hospitals, warehouses, and other forms of commercial real estate.

And I was able to work less. Over the next year, I spent very little time working after 3:00 PM. Instead, we increased our family time, and I doubled down on my after-school duties. This not only gave me time alone in the car with the three girls—basketball, volleyball, ballet, piano, math, and lacrosse—but also gave Shannon respite. And through this—month after month—a few minutes with each of them daily while in transit allowed me to develop deeper relationships with these three lovely girls who were becoming young ladies. And I thought about myself far less, because I was now able to see how far more interesting they were.

Given that funds were tight, we traveled on Marriott and AMEX points for a couple of years. To make Shannon feel safe—women need to feel secure—I prepaid the mortgage payments a year in advance and kept paying each month. This also gave me some breathing room. I highly recommend this.

I took Shannon to Cabo in 2018, where we took time together to complete the healing our marriage needed. We opened up honestly and, over time, began to enjoy each other more than ever. This led to annual trips to Cabo together since. We've also been to the Maldives, Dubai, Italy, France, Spain, and various other places throughout North America in the five years since—just the two of us. I've learned to be vulnerable—frank when I don't feel strong. She's learned to tell me when she needs rest and what activities energize her. As I write this, I just returned from a walk around the block with her to talk about retirement together. I'm also helping her launch a new business in a craft she enjoys—restoring antique quilts.

But on a personal note, I was still dealing with the mental challenges—unable to concentrate or engage in deep discussions from my surgery years prior.

THEORY: REQUIRED SACRIFICIAL VOW

Vows make men. And, of course, all vows precede sacrifice. And if you want to have a real life, vows are what will build it. The fewer, the better, but always at least one. What did I learn about my sacrifice?

Vows make men.

No one can make two vows. Either they will hate the one and love the other, or they will love the one and hate the other. And so I will only make one vow. And I will need to make the only vow with my only life. You cannot serve two masters.

No ultimate vow ultimately means no true life.

And hell.

> *From the highest vow, the performance*
> *of all other vows cascades.*

And it follows for you, that your primary vow must control your lower agreements. And that's why your free will—which powers your way toward love and evil—must be given up to a higher master. A master who is trustworthy and competent to handle the sacrifice.

When one lower promise breaks, your lower covenants may stand. But when the highest vow cracks, all your covenants shatter. For the highest vow will build your very identity. And gives your sacrifice the legitimacy and power you need for redemption and beauty in your work.

Your highest vow becomes your identity over time. For your master does make your meaning. But he also makes a life. Can you imagine what your life could become with this level of integrity?

Here's an example: For me, my solemn vows—to be a faithful husband, a trusted son, and a caring father—identified the three personas of my self. But if I had to pick one to be my highest vow it would be to be a caring father. For my girls are the joy of my parents and my wife's utmost prize. I am only a good husband and son when I'm first honoring my covenant to be a present father.

YOUR NEXT MOVES

Whose altar determines whose gift.

A proper gift cascades your life in proper order.

In Step 3, you discover your master will make your meaning. But you need to see your master. All students must see and listen. If you do not pay attention or cannot see, you were never a student and that was never your master. So to whom are your sacrifices being directed? Whatever distracted you from focusing on your higher master was your real master. It was your sick mother-in-law, your overbearing boss, your cell phone, or that unholy priest from decades ago. Or the 7-day fast so you could overcome yourself for yourself.

Your excuses are not legitimate reasons.

I wanted to eat on day six of my fast, but that was just an excuse to eat. Not a legitimate reason to break my vow to fast. So I didn't eat. But while I kept that lower vow to myself to fast, I broke my higher vow to God to be a humble father committed to living long enough to raise my kids.

Excuses are rarely reasons.

And if that is you—the false student who never learns from their fake master—you need a sacrifice. Because revelation is seeing. And seeing is becoming. And all revelation requires sacrifice. It did for Alexander the Great when he decided to kneel, and it surely means that for us today.

If you are unsure of your purpose, here's how to make a proper sacrifice:

First, look at your past three months' bank statements. Do you spend most on yourself and the payments on the debt that you were responsible for incurring? If so, you are very likely pleasing to Satan. Give more to others than you spend on yourself.

*Give more to others
than you spend on yourself.*

Second, look at your calendar for the past three months. After work, did you spend most of your time alone or distracted by screens or with people who are looking down on life? If so, you are very likely being controlled by something lower—not higher. You are aiming lower, and you need to begin again with Step 2: aiming low is the only sin.

But what about work? Many of you are hoping I'll tell you to work less. Sorry to disappoint you, but none of us are working hard enough. You have never met someone who has worked too hard on the right thing. As long as there are children to mentor, elderly in Africa to feed, and babies aborted in the West while good parents long to adopt, none of us should rest.

Resting as others suffer is selfishness.

*You have never met someone
who has worked too hard on the right thing.*

And fourth, whatever you find is blocking you from serving the master you think you chose—or killing the enemy you are meant to kill—that is your next sacrifice.

- If you are using up your funds to pay the debt service you caused then get a second job and knock it out so you can see your master more clearly.
- If you are spending too much time on screens, remove them from your bedroom for good.
- If you are consuming any sort of drug that does not have an offsetting reward greater than the risk of destroying your life by using it, quit your lunacy.
- If you are sleeping more than eight hours per night, get a wake-up system in place as I mentioned earlier in this book.

Your true masters often will look like debt, drugs, sleep, and screens. I had never been a drinker or drug user, but the others certainly tempted me. And when I began to swear off those false masters, I found my business, and my family began to return to focus. I had been nearly shattered by my actions, but redeemed by the proper sacrifice of the business which was the source of all my money and status.

And masters paint better than students.

Once you have done all this, you have hope to see. You may now be ready to make the sacrifice of your very free will to God. The unalterable gift of your every whim will become your high unifying vow. And that highest vow will put all other promises and priorities in your life in proper order if you will just get out of your own way.

Keep your future in mind when you do this, however, or all you will see is pain, heartache, and struggle from your sacrifices without seeing the upside. These frictions of life are actually the accelerating force toward real joy in a rightly ordered man like you. So keep your future in mind; you are meant for a higher purpose than mere pain avoidance.

This is what the next chapter is about. Your storms are the threshold to your higher life. We will take a look at the inversion of Homer's stormy seascape sacrifice of Agamemnon's daughter to pursue his unholy war.

If you want order in your life, instead of chaos, make the highest possible vow to the highest possible person as Master. Give Him your free will. And in doing so, you will find His beauty cascading into every other part of your life. And beauty is as good as power.

Revelation requires a sacrifice.

> **TOOL: THE ANTI-STRATEGY**
>
> It's often more important to know what you should NOT do, like a bad habit or backward attitude, than to know what to do. So, as a baby step toward the idea of sacrifice and to help you clarify your Mission, Objectives, Vision, Values, and Strategy, I want to offer you their inversion: The Anti-Strategy. Stay out of this zone at all costs!
>
> Download this tool for free at **RICKWALKER.COM/9STEPS**

Alexander the Great Commanding That the Work of Homer Be Placed in the Tomb of Achilles, an engraving by Marcantonio Raimondi, showcases a poignant moment of reverence. This Renaissance masterpiece, housed at The Met, beautifully captures Alexander's admiration for Homer's epic tales, highlighting the timeless interplay between history and mythology.

Courtesy: The Met, New York City.

View this art in full color and resolution at RickWalker.com/9steps

STEP 5

KNOW JOY REQUIRES PAIN.

*A forgiven man
is more perfect
than a perfect man
never needing
to be forgiven.*

THE SET-UP:
MATURE JOY IS ART

MATURE JOY IS like great art. Mature joy enjoys following sacrifice. In this chapter, the second in this chapter pair, we will take the pain of sacrifice we discussed in the last step and flip that pain in a very unique way. We will invert the mythological Agamemnon seascape using a historical one. And in this history from centuries ago, you and I are at sea. It's our turn. Together.

> *"Art is the queen of all sciences communicating knowledge to all the generations of the world."*
> LEONARDO DA VINCI

Because if joy is going to become anything worth having, it first takes you through pain, darkness, labor, conflict, and struggle. Without these frictions, you and I live in false childish pleasure. Let me explain.

My daughters Rosie and Lily-Kate watercolor at the dinner table in our breakfast nook. I enjoy watching them paint. The little girls sometimes run up to bed and leave their brushes, paints, and clear plastic wash water cups behind. I don't mind putting it all up. Something is soothing about rinsing off a used brush filled with life and water-based paints. The bristles bend under the running water, evicting oranges and browns to roll down my thumb as they mix for one last inky fall. We each have our falls and defeats, watering down what we once thought would be an easy life. But an easy life never ends as a good one.

When they were younger, they used the brightest reds and most hopeful greens against meandering yellows. But, like all young children with a store-bought set of paints, they must use the same brush for all colors. Using the same brush means going back to and from that little cup every time they want to change colors.

Since all the paints come from the same source set, they are all water-based. After they dip the brush into the water a few times, it always reverts to the same darkened hues. That cup of water is chaotic, stormy, disobedient, and rebellious. And sometimes it needs a trip to the sink for a rinse. Once rinsed of the murky waters, they can paint freely again.

Our struggles and strife hide the hope from us, just as the storm clouds flee as the sun threatens.

But we would never notice the sun without the darkness, nor the light hues without the darks to contrast them. Life is found in the contrast.

Life is found in the contrast.

Intellectually, a completely randomized world, and our life, should have the same degrees of blah browns and grays as that unintelligent wash water. For example, it would be a boring world where the Queen of Soul, Aretha Franklin, the Operatic Pavarotti, and rock legend Bon Jovi all only sang Southern soul music. That faux world would have no separation between the watered-down musical genres, and in that fake world, the music would always be sung in the same unstructured key. And, of course, there could never be a Grammy-night crowning because musical genius could never occur if there hadn't been any contrast between greatness and the average performer. Remember that it was the struggle of slavery that birthed soul music, as the night births the sunrise.

I don't want to live in a beautyless world without any soul or darkness. A painless world would only birth joyless lives. No. I want to live in this imperfect world where ugly hurt is confronted by lovely healing.

A painless world would only birth joyless lives.

I don't desire a world missing musical variety, redemptions, or dirty brushes in a land of canvases of simple schoolchildren. That's too boring. I want to see the atonal variations of a masterpiece resolved. We all are meant to thrive in a place where meaning rebuts meaninglessness. A place where hope has something to offer.

Think a decade into your future and imagine,

- "What if my purpose is to believe in a hidden hope beyond the pain I see, and then help others believe it as well?

- What if I knew there was a rinse coming that would clean up my mess of a life?
- What if I could then begin to paint again even truer and more maturely because I once knew what it was like to be filled with meaningless pain?
- What if the dark times of today are there to accentuate the bright hope in my tomorrow?"

We hope to see our pain redeemed for joy—the presence of any worthwhile story tells us this is our longing.

And in a great life, like a great painting, we can hope that the sun will perhaps peek out from beyond the darkness surrounding us. That same darkness brought forth not only soul, but all great music, and masterful art. And all evolved men.

THE PROBLEM: OUR THINKING

What should you learn from the pain and troubles in your life? Should you, like some of the ancient legalists, believe you are being punished by the gods? Is this karma? Should you believe in random unfairness in the cosmos?

In my work dealing with world-class families, I often see the pain and hear questions: the loss of children and parents, the loss of great loves to moral failure, the encroachment of cancers, and the punishment of egos. What sense should we make of these hurts?

It seems that these circumstantial assaults—the losses, pains, and difficulties—are similar to the natural assaults—storms, hate, and rumination. But why? Can they be solved in similar ways?

Here, I suspect it may be helpful to look to the opposite of these ugly assaults—to beauty. What makes art and music beautiful to us? Could the same attributes and relationships also turn around the ugliness in our lives to make our lives lovely?

Might a master artist's canvas and our life's painful stories be painted using the same strategy valuing contrast over monotony and joy over simple pleasure?

In the last chapter, a stormy sea disrupted the Greeks' plans to sail to Troy. Howling waves crested over their warships. It was a stormy seascape of Biblical proportions. But the commander, Agamemnon, could not calm the storms without the unholy sacrifice of his daughter. The gods would not allow a mere man to calm the waves to make war. It would not have been right.

With warring Agamemnon in mind, allow me to give you an example of how pain and joy work together in life, nature, and canvas. We will take the above ideas first written out in poetry as a prophecy, see them happen in real history, and finally painted by Rembrandt. Not for war but for peace.

THE PROPHECY:
DAVID'S SEASCAPE

The greatest masters always paint a seascape with words or brushes. David, the founder of the Judean dynasty and master harpist, wrote his 107th song a thousand years BC.

> *They that go down to the sea in ships,*
> *That do business in great waters;*
>
> *These see the works of the Worker,*
> *And his wonders in the deep.*
>
> *For he commandeth, and raiseth the stormy wind,*
> *Which lifteth up the waves thereof.*
>
> *They mount up to heaven, they go down again to the depths:*
> *Their soul is melted because of trouble...*
>
> *Then they cry unto the Helper in their trouble,*
> *And he bringeth them out of their distresses.*
>
> *He maketh the storm a calm,*
> *So that the waves thereof are still.*
>
> *Then are they glad because they be quiet;*
> *So he bringeth them unto their desired haven.*

These notes were scribed as a song for the Jewish people to memorize and pass down to their children to sing. This happened for generations of oral storytellers, as did Homer's opposite example of Agamemnon in myth. Then it happened in history to a better king who did not please the false gods because He was the true God.

Still, another King, David, the Goliath-killer, described in the passage above: one both the raiser and the stiller of the storm. One who is superior to Alexander, Agamemnon, and Artemis. He says Christ is the Master, Helper, Raiser, Stiller, and Commander of storms who delivers us to safety. A lovely statement from a harp-playing boy giant-slayer.

Real men can be both dangerous and poetic.

David's Master makes the threatening waters become opportunities for truth. The turning of threats into opportunities has always been the way of the wise.

> *The turning of threats into opportunities has always been the way of the wise.*

He wrote the sailors go to the ships. They meet rowdy waves. They cannot work the boat. They cry. The Master helps. This is the pattern of the entirety of David's royal songs. And a little like Agamemnon's inability to board his ships to get to war against Troy.

Help comes only after cries.
Cries come only after trouble.

He maketh the storm calm.
The raised waves are lowered.

Those who cried were silent.
Silence begets joy.

David's song above later births itself in history around 30 AD, and then history grandchilds the very same story onto Rembrandt's canvas. Order matters when you deal with the succession of prophets and kings.

One event: prophesied, inverted, righted, then painted into a triple analogy.

Analogies are the lubricant of arbitraging masters.

EARLY TAKEAWAYS ON PAIN

We selfishly wish for an easy life. A perfect life with easily surmountable struggles and challenges. However, just as a single-color painting is not beautiful, a perfect risk-free life can never be powerful. It's the friction that makes a real life.

Vincent Van Gogh is open about this. In 1882 the unhinged master married a prostitute and was deemed a heretic. He fell into madness and depravity. In 1885, three years into his demented life turn, he writes to his brother Theo:

> "COLOUR EXPRESSES SOMETHING IN ITSELF.
> One can't do without it; one must make use of it.
> What looks beautiful, really beautiful—is also right."

He binds color, expression, and beauty together as right, and what is right is true. Does that mean art can teach us something about the purpose of our life's downs and ups? Perhaps. So stop wishing for your life to be easier and pain-free. You need to become resilient and truth-seeking.

> "What looks beautiful, really beautiful—is also right."
> VINCENT VAN GOGH

- To be resilient means to notice the differentiation between the easy and hard paths and work: to embrace effort, struggle, and work for their own sake.
- To be suspicious of anything that looks like easy fame, quick money, or casual passion.
- To note the small joy in finding a tossed-aside idea on the ground, rinsing it off, and working for a decade to turn it into wealth.
- To discover the woven way a stranger's smile takes over their face, and stop to compliment their happiness on your busiest of days.
- To raise the best child you can, then to give her away to an immature man after college, trusting the pain of losing a daughter will turn into the joy of generations of daughters to come through her.
- To walk away from a career going nowhere, out into the unknown which might go somewhere.

On your deathbed, you will realize the hard things were usually the right things. The struggle-filled path you accepted freely was the reason you found any meaning and joy in the end. And the times you avoided an ounce of pain, you drank a gallon of regret.

*Avoiding an ounce of pain,
you will drink a gallon of regret.*

You must take what ugly selfishness you hide from the world and trade it up for a lovely challenge.

- You have to agree to the work and projects that you know in advance will bring you effort, struggle, pain, and trouble.
- Accept that you will do that important project despite all of that knowing in advance what you're embarking on.
- You have to damn the damage and accept that anything worthwhile will bring risk.
- And if your work fruits something meaningful out of your frustrating labor, it is worth it.
- And that turns your troubles into something better.

Turning around these negatives in life is called redemption. Redeeming always means trading up your inferior childish self to your master with the faith you will be remade free, as a dirty brush is rinsed off once handed over by a child to his parent.

Soul is best sung by a freedman. The pain of slavery begins to be unwound when Aretha Franklin passionately sings of triumph on Grammy night. So too, the remade man is the best type of man you can become.

**Soul is best sung
by a freedman.**

The fearful cries of the sailors on the ship to the Master Peace-Giver bring them peace and joy.

Consider how amazing your plans could turn out if you expected that fruitless work to make you stronger, like a weightlifter who works out gains from resistance. You will struggle, but you will become more antifragile.

As the clouds of your struggle hide the potential of your future self, so too did Rembrandt hide a message for you in his famous painting of David's Song of the Sea.

Courtesy: Getty Images. Corbis Historical. Photographer: Barney Burstein.

View this art in full color and resolution at RickWalker.com/9steps

THE STAGE: REMBRANDT'S SEASCAPE

It was 1633, and the Dutch artist Rembrandt van Rijn was determined to paint his first and only seascape. This story of the Galilean Sea is the same psalm that also captured King David's imagination.

Rembrandt's masterpiece is ominous. Primarily dark tones—thickened paints mountaining off the canvas—with only half a hint of color. A vertical grandeur well before abstraction was considered grand.

It was the opposite of the seascape story launching into war at Troy. And I love opposites because they remind me of healing and redemption. Do you think man will one day invent an inverting paint, one that is painted on black but cures a reflective white? That would allow art to mimic the promise of forgiveness and hope. Perhaps the night mode of today's devices is a precursor to this idea—for this is a mode that helps us see when it is dark.

Rembrandt nails the depiction of a team of fishermen fighting to stay afloat during the sinister storm. They throw up over the side, one with a knife to cut the fray. The rest hang on in panic. Their souls melt because of trouble.

The waterscape is a snapshot of the precise moment the words, *Peace, be still*, are commanded to the storm. Yes, the Master's command is directed at nature. But could that command to be at peace and be still also be directed at us? Could the command also be a blessing? Is it possible that we could take part in that command if we cry out to the Helper in our trouble too? *Peace, be still* would then be welcomed words.

The sun immediately calms, with a tip-ray of light penetrating the storm clouds, illuminating the ship of the recently awoken Sun-man who was also the Master of Rembrandt, Van Gogh, David, Alexander, and Aretha Franklin.

But two-thirds of the painting remains darker water and background. Shadowy clouds interpose an angry sky. One man on the boat, the rebel denier Peter, is illuminated as the sun breaks the darkest blight. The painting is a snapshot of the moment of the command.

A snapshot of silence...

Yin and Yang represent the dance of light invading the darkness. The Master who separated that creative wash water in the beginning, with a command, arrives. He is now commanding the storm. And, if we will listen, he redeems the chaos and frees us from the void of our lives. Paradoxically—

once again—he brings forth life from certain death. He is rinsing the murky cup as he rises from the murky boat.

Just as he once brought forth everything out of nothing. He now begins to offer the inversion: your redemption means to trade your nothing for faith in His anything.

Where you stand determines who you see. My daughters see Dad, while Shannon sees Husband, and my Mom sees Son. All true of one man. On Rembrandt's canvas, he sees and then shows one man as Master—also Power, Truth, and Love; now revealed to also be the Sun of the Greeks, Egyptians, and Hebrews. For he was sleeping, yet reigning, on a bed of wood. Speaking, yet peaceful, on a sinking lumber throne. Sitting then standing.

Because he rises, from his sleep, we witness the fire of this man, represented throughout Egyptian history as the Universal Sun, burning down all the darkness around him.

This is always what he does when he rises.

A redeeming Master burns down all your darkness.

The most lovely noncharacter of the painting, where your eye is first drawn, is the yellow. And that's no accident because joy is classically symbolized by the color yellow. So is hope. David writes:

Then are they glad because they be quiet;
So he bringeth them unto their desired haven.

How could we make this painting better?

A child first paints with light colors because the dark colors dirty up their bristles and rinse water too quickly. A novice trying to invent a better seascape here—seeing this painting and the beauty of this yellow and not knowing the mastery of art—would make a great mistake trying to replicate it as something better. They would try to embellish or make another painting with more yellow. The next revision would have still more yellow because more of the most beautiful point is always better in the eye of a novice. This is how we invent worse versions of our lives when we struggle for a glimpse of false pleasure. We think more relaxation and easy effort are the way to better times.

We forget all sunrises come out of the darkness.

However, this idiocy train would eventually end in an entirely yellow canvas. This, in the untrained artist's eye, would be his relative maximal beauty. But this all-yellow canvas would end the same way as a man who avoided the difficult work and fear and vulnerability: meaningless, passionless, dead, and forgotten.

Like a chaos-less world, only an idiot would want a waterless world (the safe opposite of the storm on the sea). For we must drink in beauty to live. Without a world of water to drink or drown, we would die. Likewise, without a world of bravery, we would die hopelessly weak cowards. Bravery maximizes our joys.

Bravery maximizes our joys.

So the amateur would be very wrong where logic leads him—to the easy life and all-yellow canvas. Logic alone never leads to beauty.

Only beauty is ever right.

Masters like Rembrandt understood that beauty in the dark hues and light contrast doesn't come from the points themselves but from the differentiation between the darkest nights and the brightest days in art and in our lives.

Beauty is best delivered by painful dissonance.

All soul music's masters know that atonality advances life-giving euphony. The major-keyed song you once happily danced to saves every minor-keyed sad song, just because we know happy songs exist somewhere. So too, beauty will save the world—while we think it's still night.

There's a blazing sun you can't see behind the blah clouds.

When the girls at home first began painting, I only refilled the reds, blues, and yellows. They never wanted the darks to dirty their wash water too soon or to darken their simple paintings. But their drawing papers later began to soak up more of the dark browns and blacky hues. They matured and then understood the importance of struggles and work, just as they do for the need for dark colors in their art. Maturity acknowledges contrast.

Rembrandt's painting shows the light that invaded atonal darkness—the fulfillment of King David's song. Chaos obeyed as the night fell because the Master ordered peace. Your master makes your meaning. And that's true for a canvas, storms, struggles, and a group of fishermen who thought they were sitting inside the boat where they worked, never realizing they were sitting for a masterpiece.

That greater-than-nature now arrived for Rembrandt. Death-threatening waters turned into an opportunity. The fishermen's boat turned the tide. Life was extracted from peril. And with it beauty.

Only because the threat exists can joy ever be heightened.

On the cover of this book Hercules' heroic physique is best seen as he struggles against the endless chaos of the Hydra, contrasted against the yellow hope he will somehow prevail.

INTERPRETATION:
THE PAINTING

Think about what kind of man you want to be known as, and ask yourself,

- "Do I want to be the man who is lucky all the time, like that all-yellow canvas, or one who has lived a real life, like that masterpiece?
- Do I want to be the weak man who lives in fear, or the strong man who is feared?
- Do I want to attract and interest people like a Rembrandt painting, or do I want to be ignored as cold and sterile?
- Who would respect me if I went after the hardest projects?
- Who could I become if I stopped living safely and embarked on an adventure?"

Homer's offer was to show us how Agamemnon begins an unholy war with unholy means. Rembrandt—master of the peace—extends an offer as well. All great storytellers always have.

Counting the men aboard the boat in his painting, I noticed the Master with thirteen disciples, not twelve. That is interesting. Weren't there always twelve disciples? Why do you think there is an extra person?

The baker—or other creator—would often add a thirteenth to every twelfth to protect himself from claims of falling short on the delivery. This was an element of trustworthiness on behalf of the creator toward the receiver. The baker's dozen.

They reel to and fro, and stagger like a drunken man,
And are at their wits' end.
Then they cry unto the Helper in their trouble...

Though we sail in gusted-up waters, his message glides to us in dark vulnerability like a black swan. Yes, we might sink. But he knows something we do not, as we live in our fear and ugliness. An unknown unknown stealthily stalks us with a hope we can only scent in the saltiness of our lives but never quite see.

The thirteenth on the boat is a self-portrait of Rembrandt floating with us in our stormy world. Like the goodwill shown by the trustworthy baker, the additional figure reflects the truth of the sun; Truth, like the Sun, is most visible to imperfect men when it is beheld as an effect on one of us. Religions and philosophies filter truths to us so we can understand. We could never understand anything divine unless filtered through song, metaphor, canvas, or story.

And a filter which refracts the light into us in refreshing ways is how a masterful idea is arbitraged into us.

Rembrandt—like Shakespeare as writer-actor and Christ as Author-Timebound Man—paints himself into that cataclysmic scene in Russ Ramsey's book on the painting.

Rembrandt is the only one looking out of the painting. He's looking for you and me. Looking out to all of us. Peering through that canvas, yellow-spotted by that peeking sun. Rembrandt peers through not only four centuries but three millennia—back through to fulfill David's prophecy, Agamemnon, and the Dao. David and Rembrandt reveal Christ. He is the Man forever symbolized by the sun deities and the Sun itself, who invaded history as the fulfillment of both philosophy and religion. And it happens within an arbitraging story so we can understand it.

Do you sense it? Right there in the pause before the sun bursts out like a billion bullets. Don't be afraid to pause; be still and know in silence. The type of reverent silence that Alexander needed when he prayed. Silence, as David's song said, comes before joy. Only the still shall know.

And in our silence, he whispers us awake.

The two-dimensional painting graces us dying men higher into a three-and-a-half-dimensional living canvas. We are mere half-dimensional beings. For that speck of time we call the present is all we have. C.S. Lewis says we have already lost the past and only have hope for the future. But what if your past could be recaptured and turned from waste to fruitfulness?

Rembrandt not only adds depth to the painting by bringing all mankind's eyes into his own, but he communicates with us, even still.

His message as he looks out at you is this: Climb aboard the stormy wooden ship for an adventure. If you respond, you reclaim the past you lost to failures and struggles and gain the hope of future redemption. You regain all the fullness of time when you have been mastered by the Master who created time. But how does it work?

And the yellows turn around to make the darkest parts of our lives serve us. The fears will be mastered.

The dozen awakened that sleeping Sun-man by screaming, "Master, we are perishing!" Our help also only responds to our cries. Pain beckons our salvation if we will aim higher.

Pain is the offer of salvation.

Then, after the storm's obedience, they conversed as the Master rested back into his kingly wooden cradle.

"Who is this that even the winds and the waves obey him?"

And there, these men notice and experience nature responding to a spoken word; the laws of physics and emotional chemistry shattered into a thousand pieces. The dark myth is unwound in Christ's light.

I'd like to think Rembrandt thought of himself as one of the twelve in fear-turned-awe. I would. We all should.

They were about to be killed by nature's storm. But they never understood hierarchy and aiming higher. Never imagined the ultimate power of the ultimate Master. Never comprehended what they proclaimed to others. Just like us when we are in the midst of a struggle. We look at the waves of hurt and embarrassing fear. Refusing to cry out for the Master. Disbelieving the cloudy cups can be rinsed anew. Seeing the storms of life. Forgetting even storms have their own purpose and their own master. Forgetting that the Sun shall one day storm all storms.

The Sun shall one day storm all storms.

So, rising out of the stormy paints, we discovered why. We foolishly thought that if we wanted to act, we would need to be able to do that act or take an unholy step to please the gods. But here, we find a truer life, which if we could ever comprehend, would light up our deepest darkness. The Master's command always carries with it the power to obey.

The Master's command always carries with it the power to obey.

And if you claim you have never been commanded and therefore do not have orders, I refer you to Step 1. If you want a purpose and need a worthy enemy: Love finds its justice in the hatred and opposition to the wrong. You—by being a member of the human race—are commanded to hate and oppose injustice.

Your given breath IS your given command.

Ask yourself:

- "Do I want light, order, and beauty?
- Am I willing to follow an ancient trail to find them?
- Could I ever believe that the old worn-out way IS the adventuresome way?
- What if that hard plodding path of the ancients is the beautiful running road leading to meaning?"

If you will obey this Master, you will see—light, order, and beauty—and get power thrown in.

If I obey this master, I will see— light, order, and beauty— and get power thrown in.

Rembrandt is looking out of the masterpiece at you: "I know you, who you really are, and it's okay to join the crew. You, too, can receive the power to obey—the peace—if you just keep your eyes fixed and heart open to the Master. Aim high to pick your master."

But only the vulnerable can become brave. You must be vulnerable to trust. And to trust is to obey.

Only the vulnerable can become brave.

We are illogical about life when we flash our credentials and knowledge. We are trying to hold on through our own talents—just as the fishermen first tried to use their talents to maneuver the boat themselves into an all-yellow scene.

Thinking we know best, we actually don't know anything at all. We don't even understand the gravity of the power within our reach, so we have no right to disrupt and panic over a storming threat miles above.

We must obey the Master to be saved from the storms. The jib must be manned by an obedient and trusting servant who will brave the storms on deck. Your mind, while focused on fear and comfort, will always remain chaotic and threatened. You must look to He who is higher and stronger if you are ever to receive deliverance.

Your mind, while focused on fear and comfort, will always remain chaotic and threatened.

But when you turn your eyes away from yourself, you begin to see Truth. You not only see the shore but perhaps even see the Sun rise up to command beauty over it.

Beauty is the inversion of evil. If you can see beauty commanded to overcome the darkness of evil with your own eyes once, then you can hope to see it again.

Beauty is the inversion of evil.

And next time, perhaps it will be your turn to rise up to speak peace into someone else's war.

For all ears and eyes demand justice, and justice requires the beauty to which David, Van Gogh, and Rembrandt beckon you still.

Beauty only comes to you once you witness a Love beyond the darkness you want more than anything else. It is the vision of The Point—where Love, Truth, and Power meet—that will pull you up and out of your fear and comfort. Your fear and comfort only lie to you.

Beauty only comes to you once you witness a Love beyond the darkness you want more than anything else.

A painting without the threat of death could never tell you about the hope of life. No one who has never risked their life has really lived. Rescued life is higher than the life never threatened.

A world without evil could never be redeemed and, therefore, would be inferior to a perfectly good world. A redeemed man is more perfect than a perfect man never needing to be redeemed. Because the redeemed man offers an example of hope to the rest of us.

Your friends, family, coworkers, and the whole world need you to be brave. The world is only redeemed when heroic men fight against evil with all the hatred they can muster because they love deeply. And picked a higher master and a worthy enemy. That's your call as well.

A redeemed man is more perfect than a perfect man never needing to be redeemed.

Here paradox reemerges. Your imperfect life made perfect is more perfect than any perfect life that was always perfect.

Restoration of your imperfect life is beautiful, a beautiful perfection.

Rembrandt offers you magical truths still. And by accepting his offer, you are pulled out of the ease and passionlessness of meaningless life, and into an invincible purpose to storm those two enemies and invade the nights of others with an armor-flash of the brilliant hope of Rembrandt. A real life of meaningful battles, hurdles, and work where the false enemies of comfort and weak pain are banished forever.

THEORY:
EASINESS BRINGS UGLINESS

Folks like us expect life to be all straight and easy. We like to invent similar all-yellow worlds that would be completely perfect without evil or death, and then foolishly wish for them. Why do we wish for ease and comfort?

> *"It's only the great masters who make such mistakes; that's perhaps the best consolation, as we're then within **our rights to hope to see revenge taken by the same creative hand**....and being left with the hope of seeing better than that in another life"*
> VINCENT VAN GOGH

Van Gogh says the same thing as David wrote: He who allows the storms also stills them. Our lone right as men is to hope to see the mistakes and storms turned into joy by Christ's hand. To see justice done. And perhaps even take part in it ourselves.

Restoration of the imperfect is beautiful, a beautiful perfection. And it's only the great masters who allow it. Redemptive hope is true beauty in texture, and if we allow it, it will rouse us out of our mental slumber. We hope to see that redemption—as we witness Rembrandt paint us into history itself. And sometimes in life, as in seascapes, pain's Redeemer approaches with an offer.

As the all-yellow canvas is not worthy of greatness because it did not have a proper master (just a novice), our story also needs texture and discord. We long for the tale of evil triumphed over by the good. Our mistakes revenged by the same creative hand that gave us the free will to cause pain and badness in the first place. And Van Gogh says we have a right to hope to see it happen.

Beauty. Justice. Discord. Invert our bad into the unfathomably brilliant good.

And everything inferior in us shall be somehow perfected as ascendant beauty advances on all our drowning hearts and we take up our full dimensionality.

*If hope exists somewhere,
it can invade anywhere.*

And I began to feel all my dimensions return. For I had accepted the gaze of a master, Rembrandt. He was calling me into a better story—a life of braving and choosing both life-threatening storms and miracles. My obedience to his call seemed to fulfill my needs: my aiming higher, accepting the right Master, and finding a worthy enemy.

A little adventure will do you some good. In fact, it may do you the greatest possible good.

You need to consider your future and ask yourself,

> *"We can ignore even pleasure. But pain insists upon being attended to. God whispers to us in our pleasures, speaks in our conscience, but shouts in our pains: it is His megaphone to rouse a deaf world.... No doubt pain as God's megaphone is a terrible instrument; it may lead to final and unrepented rebellion. But it gives the only opportunity the bad man can have for amendment. it removes the veil; it plants the flag of truth within the fortress of the rebel soul."*
>
> C.S. LEWIS,
> *The Problem of Pain*

- "What would my inner life look like if I willingly took on difficult work and impossible projects with every resource I have without excuses?
- What if I entered the difficulties and expected to emerge better and stronger?"

Who would you become if you believed my drop of hope could invade your life at the right time?

And that right time would always be after you'd want it and after you'd exhausted all your other options.

It's the pain that proves you're alive.

LIFE STRATEGY: PLEASURE

The opposite of pleasure is not unhappiness or pain.

Good masters are like good parents. They know pleasure is the great squanderer of lives. The teenager calls their parents mean because they do not want them to be happy vis-a-vis pleasure-seeking. A creature of comfort always lies—in death, deception, or both. Pleasure-seeking is only good when it is routed through the lens of pain.

Pain is your unanswerable tutor. A creative lesson shouting down your mediocrity. A megaphone you always hear.

Pain shouts down your mediocrity.

If the easy thing were the right thing, you would have already done it. When faced with either difficulty or ease, without any other direction, the only safe option is to choose to do the difficult. This is why the 9 Steps are along the narrow path, and not the wide path of common men.

If the easy thing were the right thing,
you would have already done it.

Your right and good posture for approaching the Master's purpose in your life is to seek His pleasure alone. It's the joy of a proud father in you as an obedient son or daughter. By obeying—aiming higher for a master to follow and finding an enemy to defeat—true joy in you becomes possible. And far more likely.

Not that the cosmos will give you pleasure, but it will help you look through pain to see meaningful joy is possible. And that is real hope you can hold onto.

Your joy comes from the source of your wounds.
Those wounds right and rewrite you.

Before I had a family, I could never see beyond myself. I fancied myself a future Manhattanite or Vegasite, but never a suburbanite. But as I thought about it, I realized I must see past the childish desires of sports cars, free weekends, video games, and trips with the boys—onto the higher and truer desires. Those more holy desires, the ones throughout the millennia which every great man eventually turned and hardly anyone regretted: truth, love, beauty, and brave sacrifice.

To be needed by someone who needs you and loved by someone who loves you is real life. It's really the only life. After all, only those who will attend my funeral count.

> *To be needed by someone who needs you and loved by someone who loves you is real life.*
> *It's the only real life.*

Life is only dignified in your service to others who need you. And if no one needs you, you have yet to discover real life. You receive it as you take up anticipated friction and hurt for the possibility of love. Life is the taking up of anticipated pain for love. This exchange offers you a woodstove-warmed rustic cabin on the side of a remote mountain. Only a fool trades that for a cold concrete box in a city to live and die alone.

> *Life is the taking up*
> *of anticipated pain for love.*

And to take on temporary pain willingly saves you the eternal pains thrust upon you. For instance, when I chose to begin rising at 3:30 AM to get to the office to begin my enlightenment, that was painful. I struggled to get to sleep the night before. But eventually, I was tired enough to go straight to sleep. My willingly accepted struggle overtook the easy thing that had been missing evenings with my family to work late.

You'll sleep if you work and live hard enough.

> *You will receive temporary pains willingly,*
> *or eternal pains forcibly.*

> "We are not cabin-dwellers, born to a life cramped and confined; we are meant to explore, to seek, to push the limits of our potential as human beings. The world of the senses is just a base camp: we are meant to be as much at home in consciousness as in the world of physical reality."
>
> VED VYASA,
> *The Bhagavad Gita*

The only way to be satisfied with yourself is through difficult work and voluntary discomfort. You will never respect yourself without it. Respect from others never arrives otherwise.

My loss of sleep to rise earlier than I wanted was tough. The loss of my low-aimed singlehood dreams, Congress, power, Manhattan was painful if I do not look to the other side of the scale. If the voluntary struggle is best, then the love on the other side of the scale will more than balance. And it does. My wife and kids tip over all those fleeting vague promises. And that choosing to do the hard thing begins to make a good life.

INTERPRETATION: YELLOW SWEET TEA

After elementary school, I would go over to my Grandma's house for a few hours while my parents finished working. I sat in one of the two recliners and ate some amazing Italian food. My PaPa, a lifelong plumber, always sat in the other recliner after a day's hard work with his yellow cup of iced sweet tea.

After firing cannons in the Korean War, he lost most of his hearing. I went through his military records after he passed away to find out he went AWOL from Korea to travel back to San Antonio to see my Grandma. He was fearless. Growing up on a farm as an outcast adopted child, he was brutally beaten and then forced to sleep in rattler-infested chicken coops when they were sick of him. He was fearless because he had already been forged by life.

And I recall PaPa sitting at the Thanksgiving dinner table with his ordinary translucent yellow cup enlightening the color of his rich, dark sugared sweet tea. Yellow is the color of joy.

And there, a mostly deaf, tortured man sat in the presence of his loving family, sipping on a cup representing wrath-turned-joy. Thankful for the joy he would have missed if he had lived an easy life. The cup reflected his life's story of joyful struggle drunk into his own body as a healing salve. He sat drinking in his life's joy with his eyes—his loves—to redeem his suffer-filled past. His joy was seen around that table. For sweet joy always comes served up with darkness. Don't underestimate the yellow. Or the wrongs you suffer.

Of course, a yellow translucent cup filled with dark sweet tea is a little like Rembrandt's brilliant yellow against a dark background of painful storming waves. This is how true joy always becomes known—in contrast to difficulty.

You will never be thankful for your blessings because you never notice them without first struggling.

And I've found that just noticing the curious coincidences often makes life better.

*The thanking is why
you receive blessings.*

And this is how it will be for you. But what does this mean? Should you be the punching bag of a man so that you can hope for something better?

YOUR NEXT MOVES

Now it's your turn to take a step or two. It's you who will need to decide what lessons and theories will sail and which to toss over the side.

First, understand that every threat you see is an opportunity for someone. Perhaps for you. Even someone else's threat may be an opportunity for both them and you. An opportunity to help and be shaped, perhaps.

That's how the economy works. When I go to the store to buy a bag of potatoes, it is an expense for me, but it is income for the store. My expense (a negative) is the store's income (a positive). But my expense in buying that bag of potatoes is only negative if I don't do anything with them and allow them to sit and spoil.

Now, if I take those potatoes home and make some potato soup for my kids, we will flip that expense (like we can flip a threat and a pain). That expense to my bank account is turned into an investment in my family. The expense (a small but still negative thing) becomes a meal for my family (a positive thing). And if I teach my kids around that dinner soup, even while they paint, I have a massive opportunity I would not have accessed before had the negative (threat, pain, expense) never occurred.

I've found that when I go to the store and purchase (expense) what I want, it is always better than being forced to eat whatever is molding in the pantry. Buying from the store at a higher price is a worthy arbitrage than farming potatoes for myself to save a few bucks. We must pick our pains, challenges, and investments, or we will be handed the fate of whatever.

So you must pick a challenge, like an enemy, and direct your efforts to the challenges and pains you choose. You must make investments you determine are highest, or everything will be eaten away by inflation. You must choose the trade-offs that allow you to (Step 1) best defeat your chosen enemy and (Step 3) serve your master well.

But what does pain have to do with enemies and masters?

It is your pursuit of a worthy master and worthy enemy that will determine the outcomes of your pains, threats, challenges, and chaos. It's the pursuit that Rembrandt invites you to join him in.

How the hell does that work?

It's the quality of the target of your pursuit that will flip your threats into opportunities. Not you.

Your target enemy and master will turn your mediocre life into a life lived on the redemptive miracle-laced ship where the Master is.

- You'd never know He was good if you didn't see him shout down evil.
- You'd never know he was light without banishing the darkness.
- You'd never known such a thing as hope existed if you had never experienced a risk.
- You'd never believe in light if you had never first experienced darkness.

It's not about your effort. It's about your master's quality.

Real joy lives on the edge where the storms have been commanded, and the darkness is maximally ugly and destructive. But if you will look out through the driving rain, a hint of yellow hope is on the horizon. A drop of hope anywhere means redemption is possible everywhere. Hope threatens all your dark struggles.

*A drop of hope anywhere means
redemption is possible everywhere.*

The fearful man in the boat first sees the sunrise. The beaten boy kept in the chicken coop is the first to rise with the roosters. The yellowing of his dark bruises sends a glimmer of hope that healing is on the horizon.

Hope threatens all your dark struggles.

In the next chapter, we will explore the unknown beyond the horizon. There your vulnerabilities become the seeds of something you would never expect: world-shattering power.

For now, trust your darkest times will paint your brightest life.

> **TOOL: THE PERPETUAL ACTION LOOP**
>
> I've found there are six primary ways to turn your strategic actions into game-changing routines. These powerful tactics will work together, or independently, to bring lasting change: to reinforce your Strategies and enforce your Anti-Strategies. And fulfill your life's Vision and Mission.
>
> Download this tool for free at **RICKWALKER.COM/9STEPS**

PAIR C:
OUR MINDSET

> "But what manner of people will have the wherewithal to guard such a state, and what virtues will they need to possess if they are to fulfill their role as guardians?
>
> "Certainly they must have a spirited, even savage nature if they are to defeat the enemies of the city, but then they must also be gentle and loving if they are to be a blessing and not a curse to their fellow citizens."
>
> **PLATO**
> *The Republic*

The Rehearsal of the Ballet Onstage by Edgar Degas, housed at The Metropolitan Museum of Art, captures the elegance and rigor of ballet dancers in rehearsal. Degas' mastery of pastel and composition highlights the dynamic interplay of movement and stillness, embodying the grace of 19th-century Parisian theater culture as seen from the orchestra pit.

Courtesy: The Met, New York City.

View this art in full color and resolution at RickWalker.com/9steps

STEP 6

EMBRACE THE UNKNOWN.

*Nothing certain
will lead to wealth,
love, or relevance.*

THE SET-UP:
FLYING SWANS & LYING STATS

Let me show you the unexpected upside of unpredictability in your life. This third chapter pair—Steps 6 and 7—reorients our thinking. In this first of the pair, we will see how power forms in a manner none of us would have ever invented: power's opposite. And in the next chapter by looking at two of the most competent men who have ever lived: President George Washington and Secretary Ben Carson. Their lives—the first of fatherly tyranny and the second of skillful purity—help us discover the treasuries hiding in our fear and vulnerability, to empower competency we need to defeat the evil problems all around us. This new path to a masterful life is now accessible for regular guys like you and me.

The real world is full of paradoxes where both ends of the spectrum are not only true, but they even produce their opposites. Let's begin with the worlds of intellectual statistics and imaginative ballet.

I noticed this trend about fifteen years ago on reality television. A couple claimed "I love you" when the relationship matured to safety. However, we now tell each other, "I think I've fallen for you." Do you see what has happened? Society's suspicion of love's eventual demise has replaced our hope of that love. Once a positive hope, our love has been turned into a negative fear.

Our suspicions betray us. Our off-the-cuff projections about life's great pursuits rob us of relevance. So we consider love as just a feeling instead of an eternal force.

And that's how we lose what should be kept.

We cannot trust the known and expected events based on the past to predict the patterns of future human action, economics, stories, or even heroics. We have to embrace that unknowableness about our world and others.

I engulfed a little book in a single afternoon in my thirties while sitting at the pool in Mexico with Shannon. Sun shining and beef fajita nachos sizzling—American style—plated on my towel-covered lounger. The read was a rare work on the unreliability of statistics on relevant global events. Its findings on how significant events work enlightened my darkening mind and helped me catch up to my hopeful heart. (Dark, because I was still focused on the wrong things.) *The Black Swan*, by Nassim Nicholas Taleb, is the quintessential work on relevance. Understanding relevance was crucial if I wanted to live a relevant life. But how could my life become relevant?

Taleb argues that we create our fallacy by incorrectly trying to predict the future based on past observations of the normal.

We falsely believe in mankind's linearity and predictability—even genius. We swallow the sweet medicine of a bell curve normal distribution on a graph and end up sickening with repeated bad decisions. Taleb proves that normalizing impact, relevancy, trends, and expectations based on the past are wrong and deceptive. And falsehood becomes evil when we consent to deception. So, trends are unreliable predictors because they don't matter in the grand scheme. Relevance deals with the grand schemes of our world.

> *Logical causation is too weak to dignify us.*

Our unknown remains unknown because we look for trends. Trends are mere averages without outliers. But the outliers impact us more than the averages. So, it's irrational to look to statistical trends and averages to make major decisions.

How do I know this beyond what the statistician Taleb is telling me? I know this because I've found love is our greatest driver, yet love is neither rational nor statistically predictable. Honest love, however, is true and relevant. And solid. So, we have something strong and real that does not conform to predicables or statistics living inside us. Unmanufacturable.

THE SUB-LESSON:
TRENDS DON'T MATTER

The most impactful events are the outliers. Outliers are the least predictable because they do not fit on the trend curve of the averages (called the Gaussian curve). They aren't what we would predict based on past observations, but frame our reality.

Humanity lives off-guard. Mankind cannot prepare for the presumed unknowable. Yet the unknowable and unpredictable happens. This is what moves the world statistically.

Taleb's Black Swan is about the unexpected and improbable. Major events move the world, not the millions of common events we can plot on a graph.

Black Swan events—the unexpected, unknown, outliers—have three components:

1. These events could not have been expected based on the historical knowledge in the space.
2. They are only explainable after they pass. The speed of the 2004 Asian tsunami was too fast to comprehend the cause while it was happening.
3. They must have had an extraordinary impact. The magnitude of their weight must shift the domain, tilting world history.

I already knew mere causality was beneath man's dignity. It was clear we are more than calculators wearing skin. But now, the shock: causation and statistical probability are shown to be incorrect predictors of anything significant if based on the past. The trends don't matter in the long run.

Most of what matters to us—the meaningful stuff—is beyond the protection of mathematics and often wrapped in a way that looks strong but is vulnerable underneath. This idea is from Taleb, a statistician.

And how applicable is it that the chapter that dealt with pain, struggles, and difficulties bringing joy is now followed by a chapter about the potential hiding in your weakness? You deserve some opportunity. And perhaps it will look a bit like devastation and pain at first.

So great events invade our lives through the vulnerabilities of the events that were once thought mighty. Unknown events invading known events. And in a certain sense, an unknowable power invading an unsuspecting vulnerability is a Black Swan event.

HOW DO I BUILD A LIFE THAT MATTERS?

So, how do you build a life that matters? The average is what you see and measure every day, but the unmeasured unknown is what will move the future. That is relevant.

Could it be a contrarian strategy? Should you just do the opposite of what the majority is doing, and you'll be fine? Or does that only work in investing for certain people?

Because I wanted to help you build a life that really matters, I needed to figure out a way to identify what is truly relevant and learn from it. I would be the student. And students must learn about what they don't know.

To see something unknown, I would have to look for major events that shook the world—Black Swan events. But more than that, I would need to look for an odd little characteristic that would be shockingly central to that powerful event: vulnerability.

I would need to seek out vulnerability. Would I begin with the great literature or historical figures? No. Like Christ, I would begin with those around my supper table.

MINDSET-SHIFT: TCHAIKOVSKY & SWANS

I have three daughters, and in my home I just wish to be considered one of the girls. My oldest, Emerson, is a pre-professional ballerina. She is an astonishing blend of artistry and competency.

As Emerson's skills develop, so does her poise. As her talent matures, so does her loveliness in the dance. Skill, beauty, and form meet. They collide in fragility—in vulnerability. The en pointe ballerina soloist can never be more vulnerable because she has her entire weight and balance on the tip of a single toe. She is neither footed nor stable, let alone sure-footed.

Or more lovely.

As vulnerability and complexity increase in life and business, so does the potential for disaster. But as the potential for disaster matures, so will a story's depth. This is the theme of all the great plays and relevant lives: our greatest disasters just may bring forth our most treasured moments. And if we are paying attention, those moments can remake our lives.

It was 1877 Russia. The musical master Pyotr Ilyich Tchaikovsky was tasked with composing his first ballet, *Swan Lake*, to be performed by Moscow's Bolshoi Ballet. But it was a colossal failure because the choreography was undanceable for the ballerinas trying to match their movements with his musical mastery.

Tchaikovsky handed Moscow's ordinary choreographer his arrangement of complex genius to interpret. Any interpreter must know where he begins and how to get where he needs to go. A genius does not care about the plottable chart of the ordinary averages because he lives in the outliers.

> *Genius and mediocrity cannot coexist.*
> *One always destroys the other.*

Later, in 1895 St. Petersburg, two norm-shattering choreographers, Petipa and Ivanov, ascended. Tchaikovsky's *Swan Lake* music was reimagined for ballet. Their visual interpretation displayed harmonic majesty. The unknown greatness of Tchaikovsky's music—once only heard—was now seen in the dance. The paper music manifested in flesh.

But it was two years late. Tchaikovsky last drew breath in 1893. He died a failure in this endeavor into ballet. His brilliant composition was performed too soon.

Order matters. He never knew that he had become the most famed and performed ballet composer in the world.

An ordinary man cannot transliterate the extraordinary. But an extraordinary genius like Tchaikovsky—or Bach—will leap through the centuries to find the proper interpreter (translator, mediator, choreographer). That is relevant.

The confluence of greats is rare. The world is never big enough. Ask Julius Caesar and Pompey. The more dominating the intelligence, the rarer its fulfillment in time. Ask Dante and Beatrice. Ask Plato and Aristotle. Ask Michael Jordan and Dennis Rodman.

Genius requires imagination to be aimed at relevance. Genius and imagination must come as a pair to be known and relevant. And that's why Step 2—to aim high—is an obvious choice for genius.

Intelligence with irrelevant imagination is a squandered tragedy. Ask Einstein. Ask Gandhi. Ask Kahneman and Tversky.

Why do world-great geniuses aim at efforts, problems, or events of relevance instead of the ordinary?

Allow me to provide a triple analogy to reveal how we interact on the edge of vulnerability and power.

INTERPRETATION: SWAN LAKE

I spent my college years playing trumpet in bands, ensembles, and orchestras, taking music theory, conducting, and orchestration classes, so I learned a little about music.

Emerson knows the choreography of the dance, and I know a little about the orchestration.

The orchestration of *Swan Lake* features the oboe, which falls into the rare classification of a double-reeded woodwind. Woodwinds sound when lips blow through vibrating wood. A saxophone and a clarinet, two of the most common instruments, are single-reeded. They are common because, in part, single reeds are easier to control.

But, the double reeds of the oboe are rare. Oboes are never-tamed beasts. The oboist blows into the thinnest imaginable wooden straw which needs precise re-moisturizing minute-by-minute. The oboe demands facial, abdominal, and mental focus, like the ballerina. The slightest relaxation of concentration will damn the entire orchestra. The oboist is as vulnerable as a swan or a toe-tipped ballerina.

And remember: all Black Swan events arrive through vulnerability.

Swan Lake's orchestration needed to feature the most vulnerable oboe because, after all, it is the story of the en pointe (toe-tip) ballerina—exposed, alone, and afraid on stage.

The ballerina and the oboe have a single chance at triumphant grandeur enfolded in the potential for devastation. That's their ordinary existence. As is the existence of the lovely swan upon the hunter-prone water.

The en pointe ballerina: the most vulnerable soloist.

The oboe: the most vulnerable of all the instruments.

The swan: the most vulnerable of all the animals.

All three are unsurpassed in powerful grace while never more at risk of tragedy. *Swan Lake* was originally authored as the written story *The Stolen Veil*. The images of the ballerina, the oboe, and the swan depict the complexity of love in that story.

In the ballet, Odette, the true love, wears a white tutu because Odile, the false love, must symbolically wear a black one. All children understand that. It's only right. When performed as a live Tchaikovsky ballet, you can see it. Those in the gallery first see the truth about identity: true love is wearing white.

Beyond the stage and the costuming, the technical brilliance of choreographic imagination beautifies the natural sophistication of Tchaikowsky's orchestration. You must have both.

And this is how the world works—and how a triple analogy often unfolds in Black Swans.

The ballerina hears the oboist's song without seeing the oboe. The oboist hears the ballerina's toetaps above without viewing her dance. The visual and the auditory are in tandem, without direct communication. But how?

The Maestro can see and hear both the ballerina and the oboist and acts as an interpreter (mediator). He sets the tempo. The tone. The motion of the music. The conductor coordinates passion. He's an actor who leads the cast with his back to the audience. He commands responsive repose.

A bit too fast, the ballet falls into disarray.

A smidge slow, the ballerina's turns become falls.

The fortissimos become mezzo forte.

Energy dies.

The grace of a ballerina is not found in her feet but in her hands. The hands are free to dance when the feet must work. Emerson taught me this without saying a word.

The fairness of the oboe is not found in the notes but in the vibrato's sweetness. Only the vibrato is unchained from the score's shackles. Choose your maestro.

The hands of the ballerina.

The vibrato of the oboe.

The contrast between true and false lovers.

The power reaches the hearts of the audience through these hands, vibrato, and contrasting loves.

A ballet without a conductor is passionless chaos.

The train without tracks derails.

The lady without discretion dies alone.

The boy who never does his chores becomes a disgrace to his own boy one day.

A cocked crossbow of the Princely hunter nearly kills the white swan which he intends to love forever.

As the ballerina and the oboe, the swan is most lovely when vulnerable to loss. But what does this mean for us?

How does this vulnerability in an oboe, ballerina, and swan impact your pursuit to discover relevance? What does it mean for the man wandering and looking for something to hang his hat on?

You need to consider your future and ask yourself,

- "What if I could embrace the unknown of what could happen if I went all-in on one project?
- What could I become if I went all-in on life and honestly tried to find and develop a little love for someone other than myself?"

THEORY:
LOVE REQUIRES VULNERABILITY

Love is our most-valued loss. For love IS loss. Loss of our wants. Loss of our defenses. Loss of our offensive shaping and correcting the other person to be a proper adult. Instead of allowing them to see our true vulnerabilities.

To lose the desire to overcome them to instead be overcome BY them—that is real love. Love requires vulnerability. That is how the power gets into us. If it is true love, it is also the most unplottable, unguessable gain.

Love requires vulnerability.
That is how the power gets into us.

_____

No one receives love without vulnerability because no love exists without the potential for loss. True love only comes from openness to another. As we know from Step 5—all joy requires vulnerability to pain.

If we play, our eyes must be on the maestro and the music. If we dance, our rhythm must be with both the music and our position on the stage. Our indifference to our work and life dreams will turn us meaningless and mediocre.

My campaign's uncaring weeks of labor and hate will strip away months of my purposeful intentions.

The ballerina paints with her hands what lives within her soul.

Only the vulnerable see real beauty. Only the vulnerable are strong enough to look. The vulnerably lovely are so unexpected to us and attractive to invading power that these Black Swan events revolutionize the world.

Our true purpose is to give away love: to empty ourselves for our neighbors, coworkers, kids, and friends. That means choosing them over everything else every time. Being present, not just there.

Our selfish hope is to be loved and to collect friends as trinkets. Our false security, in our politicians, friends, freedom, and money, turns what is meant to be a positive hope—to be loved—into a negative one—not to lose the accolades we receive from relative strangers.

Love must get near enough to shoot us.

Love's not a function of the quantity of friends, but rather the enduring quality of the love.

I've found that if I was authentic enough with Shannon and my three girls, I would participate in, no reflect, a better and richer love than a million friends could ever offer.

For a million likes could never match a single love.

A million likes could never match a single love.

I falsely believed needing love was being needy. So, I posed as a cold, strong man when the authentically warm father can best give and receive. And I would soon find out that a strong man can never be vulnerable. Only a vulnerable man can be invaded by strong power or true love.

Power takes up residency in honest vulnerability.

Vulnerability is not only lovely, but it is also right.

YOUR NEXT MOVES

And so we return to where we began: You and I both need more unpredictability in our lives. We need an adventure to call our own. We need to put ourselves out there and know that we don't know how it will turn out.

You see, knowing that you don't know something is always the first step to growth and wisdom. You must embrace that vulnerable position as a student before you can learn from your master. Aiming high means you know you are below. And that's a darn good start. And it often looks like humility.

It is not the averages and trends that are relevant; it is the outliers that do not fit the graph. These Black Swan events bring relevance, yet you ignore them because they bear the curious notion of failures, miracles, and vulnerability first. But don't ignore the vulnerability.

The obvious question here is: what does the master you serve have to do with a Black Swan event? Aren't events and people two different categories? Aren't power and vulnerability opposites? Some of that is a paradox. Paradox is the highest form of truth where we will arrive soon.

The more important question should be: what do you really know?

If the Black Swan event (the unknown unknown) is not shocking enough, consider this: one event can wipe out all statistical predictability. This fact alone renders all your knowledge useless—none of it can be trusted. Unless the source of that knowledge and wisdom is behind all Black Swan events. Sometimes, Step 2 means to aim higher you must look back AND BEHIND.

The destruction of your old life's facts becomes your new wisdom. Forcing you to go back and look behind all the great events that shook the world. This master source of all the great religions, philosophy, art, and music has also shaped the world just as it has shaped all of literature if you track the sources of the great works.

Your hopes, plans, and very tomorrows are each shattered by any Black Swan event, if you are not aiming at the now-unseen Maestro directing all world-shattering and world-forming happenings.

The unknown is more important than the known.

When you don't know, you can either admit your weakness or subvert progress for your pride. Weakness seeks to fill the void. Pride caverns you in on yourself.

But, the greatest imaginable Black Swan event would offer you the most disproportionate upside payout for the bet made. It's also the safest bet when the infinite upside (a forever-freeing resurrection) is calculated against the finite downside (a temporal slave's death).

Oh, and this greatest imaginable Black Swan event would have the greatest picture of the most vulnerable man in the most vulnerable of positions ascending to the most powerful place and there seen to unshatter all true victims. And revenge his hand against ravaging time.

Decision-avoiders live a hell on earth. Hell is occupied with those who abandon reason for fear. Those fear-filled ballerinas are flat-footed; they never dance en pointe. The composer's music is never choreographed and, therefore, never danced out of fear of failure. Your life will be hellish if you avoid failure and vulnerability.

To be a complete man, you will retain reason with that passionate fear. Your intellect is intertwined with your imagination. Your hope can be threaded with trust. And that makes you a relevant man. And dangerous.

Failure is a requisite for greatness.

I suspect this intertwined whole man is who you want to become. Though vulnerable because you retain the child-like curiosity that you don't know anything, in reality, you need both your intellectual mind and your imaginative heart. The composer and the choreographer need one another, as Emerson and I as well do. The music fathers the dance. The willing vulnerability, the power.

Only the humble may discover the uninventable unknown because only the humble will know to look for what they need.

Only the humble are strong enough to allow their lying (statistics-based) reality to be shattered into a billion pieces so it might reassemble in truth (Black Swan-guided reality). In light of the discovery of the unknown. For all known first begins unknown. The mastery of all masters is sourced in a single Master. And He only shows us a single step and a single note at a time. The Maestro's hidden in the pit now but is rumored to ascend the stage when the ballet is complete.

Nothing certain will lead you to wealth, love, or relevance. And that's why you must throw away what is certain and accept the risk of the unknown. And nothing is more unknown than a Black Swan event that's about to happen.

So, I wish to share with you three risks you must take to find meaning in three key parts of your life: wealth, love, and relevance.

1. **Wealth:** All investments and businesses are predicated on taking a chance. If everyone is already doing it, you are too late. Until you build your wealth, you should go all-in on one industry you can understand but one that also has a pending correction no one fully detects. And when you detect that vulnerability, look for the point of investment entry where the most asymmetric upside intersects

with a capped downside. Even investing everything you have is capped, if you only go back to zero.

2. **Love:** To love someone, you must admit you need them. And, like the ballerina, oboe, and swan, that is a vulnerability. But it may be paired with beautiful love which may be the strongest force in the universe. But to receive love, you must be open to losing yourself in that love as well. How else would the love get into you if the pain had not revealed love's path?

3. **Relevance:** Recall Step 2—your master makes your meaning. That is true here—your master's relevance limits your meaning. And the best master will always be loved, which requires you to be vulnerable to admit you need him and be willing to receive his life and wisdom.

But here's the catch: a strong enough master does not need your love. Or you. Yet, he will want both.

> *The most relevant master will not need you but will hunt you because he knows you need to be needed.*

And somehow, picking the right master aligns with relevance. He throws in the love, just enough resources, and the wisdom you need to fight your worthy enemy. It would never be proper for wisdom to give you insight without throwing in love and wealth as well. The baker always throws in an extra for those who asked for a dozen, but only after the oven first burns out the vulnerable imperfections.

> *It would never be proper for wisdom to give you insight without throwing in love and wealth as well.*

So, their ramifications multiply as the Black Swan events continue in your world. The bell curve model of your observation-based averages and predictions lies on the world's concert stage floor in defeat. Scientism and mediocrity as dumb idols lie in open repose. Casketed, yet worshiped.

While a thousand towering events go unnoticed in the chanting Christmas choir behind.

These unpredictable and unknown Black Swan events tower over reality and are truly relevant. They move the world, just like a false political poll, and rainfall an hour away flooded away my life before it brought me into this better life. But to look up, we must look behind these events to their source—to their master—to the Master defining all relevance. And maestroing all hearts and all real love.

Love is accepted in the rejection of likes. Truth is accepted in the rejection of mere facts. The highest Maestro is only accepted if you reject all the lower brutes in the audience tapping their feet off-beat.

You can never look for truth unless you retract your eyes from that which is false. And there, in accepting and rejecting, you find a worthy life of adventure.

> *You can never look for truth unless you retract your eyes from that which is false.*

You must embrace the unknown master before you're ready. Or worthy.

That's how love begins, after all: an unknown premature sacrifice with the hope of finding relevance in the other person.

Power and vulnerability intersect if you aim high enough beyond the averages.

You will find your true way in the rejection of the false path. You may find a black swan if you stop only expecting white swans to exist. You may discover the supernatural if you stop demanding only the natural exists.

And, paradoxically, only in recognizing your false beliefs can you look away from falsehood toward truth. Only what you give to others can be kept. In the next chapter, we will look at the unknowable paradox of finance, love, and salvation: nothing you have not given away will ever be yours.

And I suspect the greatest possible Black Swan event would have something to do with the lowest possible overcoming the most powerful by giving away the most valuable to the least deserving.

The greatest possible Black Swan event occurs as the lowest possible individual overcomes the most powerful evil by sacrificing the most valuable good for the most vulnerable.

———

But for now, go climb a mountain. Mount a stage. Go into the other room and hug your family for no reason at all. Embrace the unknown. Accept a little adventure in your life.

The Golden Age is a vibrant oil painting from 1605-1610, epitomizing Mannerist elegance. The idyllic scene depicts nude figures in harmony with nature, evoking mythological themes of innocence and abundance. This masterpiece, part of The Met collection, showcases Wtewael's intricate detailing and dynamic composition. Taken from the opening pages of the classical author Ovid's *Metamorphoses* (8 CE), which describes a time before the ages of silver, bronze, and iron when "spring was everlasting ... streams of sweet nectar flowed," and mankind, "without a law," did right and lived contentedly.

Courtesy: The Met, New York City.

View this art in full color and resolution at RickWalker.com/9steps

STEP

7

GIVE AWAY
WHAT YOU
WANT TO KEEP.

You lose what you try to keep.
You only eat what you plant.

THE SET-UP: COMPETENCY

You deserve to lose what you try to keep.

I'm not very political anymore, but I've found many of the greatest givers, and tyrannical takers, are drawn to public service. Very few are competent. Shannon and I were honored to be invited to the 70th birthday party of the U.S. Secretary of Housing and Urban Development (2017-2021), Dr. Ben Carson at Mount Vernon. Weeks earlier, we hosted a fundraiser for his education nonprofit, American Cornerstone Institute, at our place outside Houston on his wife Candy's birthday. We remembered her vegetarian birthday cake.

He is one of the most caring individuals and the most competent. I always take note when I see competence and compassion meet in the same individual. So should you.

Dr. Carson holds sixty honorary doctorates and successfully conducted the first separation of conjoined twins as the world's top pediatric neurosurgeon—serving for 30 years at the Johns Hopkins Children's Center, including time as Director of Pediatric Neurosurgery. He was a 2008 Presidential Medal of Freedom honoree and an 8-time best-selling author. You may have seen the movie *Gifted Hands*, which is about his life. Cuba Gooding, Jr portrayed him.

Dr. Carson is competence. Not the little league pitcher who grew up to start some company with a hundred employees. Competence requires world-class execution across multiple domains. Oh, and he and his wife funded dozens of libraries in inner-city schools. Maybe hundreds more none of us will ever find out about.

Arriving at his birthday party, after a 45-minute drive from D.C. proper, in a splurged Uber black, we stepped out for quite the evening. Me in my dark blue tuxedo and Shannon in a dark gray evening gown, we glided the earliest American history paths up to the main museum. The wafting flowering trees laid down a pattern of white and pink against the green lawns. A younger and cockier self would have missed it all.

Expecting a thousand people for such a major event, we were shocked to be two in a crowd of 150—well out of our social league. We were the only attendees who were not ambassadors, governors, presidents, or members of the presidential cabinet. There was only a single lowly member of the U.S.

Congress there, with whom we met for drinks later that evening back at the hotel to compare notes.

Shannon doesn't care who you think you are—she treats everyone the same, and because of that, people are just drawn to her in a special way. She's a magnet.

After dinner, the party relocated to the greens overlooking the Potomac, ornamented with standing tables, staffed bars, and dessert presentations, including a replica birthday cake of Mount Vernon. A string quartet bounded Mozart and Bach against political chatter. The scent of the bubbly poured freely, mixed with the richness of the custom perfumes to cling inside my nostrils. Glamour was real. Our eyes drawn to the elegant gowns. Shannon whispered the designer names in my ear.

I fetched drinks and desserts, leaving her alone at a cocktail table. Walking back, I was pleased to see that another couple joined us. Shannon spoke with the wife but ignored the husband.

I couldn't shake the feeling as I approached in the now ten o'clock darkness: I recognized the husband from somewhere. And, of course, as soon as I set down the drinks to introduce myself, I realized it was the former Secretary of Homeland Security—ignored by the ladies. His humility cloaked his competence. But why was he giving them his attention and not vice versa?

After the fireworks show, we took the opportunity to privately tour Washington's old estate to learn more about his personal and public life. A fascinating place boasting his humanity. Mount Vernon showed not only Washington's fatherliness but also his propensity for rottenness when I heard of his slaves. It reminded me of the duality of us all—saints or sinners—often both simultaneously. Washington was saving us while enslaving others. We wish we only got the good George and the bad never happened. But that's not ever reality unless you want an invented reality.

Men never arrive whole—we only come broken.

I asked Shannon why she ignored the husband on the drive back into D.C. She quipped, "The wife looked more important." Wives usually are.

However, the appearance of power, like that of George Washington or a member of the President's Cabinet, is always less than what you would have expected. Appearances can deceive. But results rarely do.

Eventually, you become the product of your competency and integrity.

*You become the product of
your competency and integrity.*

THE PROBLEM:
RELEVANCE AND POWER

Isn't founding a country an unusually important thing to do? It's certainly on the list of things that could be considered relevant. So founding the greatest of all the countries might be one of the most competent actions. And doesn't that come from a collection of power and resources?

But what kind of man was Washington? Surely a tyrant to do such a thing, right? His detractors will cite his slaves, his wartime threats, and perhaps his wielding of America's claims without protecting Native American territory. Washington was not woke.

Why do the most pathetic people in my life who accomplished the least always tell me power is wrong? Why is it them who say wealth requires greed? These are the people who have the saddest lives saying it. And the ones who spend everything on themselves.

We confuse power with wrong. We make this mistake because we assume power requires a nefarious intent: to self-serve, benefit, or be served. We think all power is power OVER, and not empowerment TO.

Instead, in researching George Washington, I found something nearly the opposite. This man perhaps did the most visible Black Swan type of thing: Washington took away the most-treasured territory (America) from the most potent military (British) only to then set The United States on track to become the most dominating force on the planet.

But why do you think it worked? Was it luck? You know better. It took competence, integrity, and hard work.

Success must be built. Marathons take steps. Years take days.

But only the competent and love-directed who don't seek power deserve it.

WASHINGTON AND CARSON

In 1732, this greatest leader, fathering the greatest country, was born in Virginia.

At age six, it is said George Washington wielded his brand new ax on a fruit tree. Eventually, his hacking killed the tree. When examined by his father, he famously quipped: I cannot tell a lie. And for telling the truth, little George is praised for his honesty instead of punished for his actions.

Washington entered military service, eventually rising to the role of commander of all troops in Virginia. Despite being nearly killed multiple times, including two horses shot from under him, plunged into icy rapids to nearly freeze while pursued by an enemy army, and his clothes shot up by four additional bullets without injury, he prevailed. He was a divinely protected man.

As he led his first army of over 1,000 men, paid at his own expense as a personal gift to his country, he gained national glory. Eventually, he became one of the seven delegates to the first Continental Congress.

When the colonies sought a commander-in-chief for all the military forces, Washington recommended General Andrew Lewis for the post. When Washington was finally chosen as commander at the Second Continental Congress in May of 1775, he was said to have declared his own unfitness for the position before reluctantly accepting.

This meekness of Washington reminded me of Dr. Carson's demeanor—humble competency delivering results.

Dr. Carson's historical separation of conjoined twins required humility. Despite his dozens of doctorates, he chose to travel all over the world to learn how to preserve both childrens' brains while stopping blood flow to them to operate. He literally froze their blood and stopped their hearts. And he knew after an impossible procedure, he would have to bring these children back to life—literally. He humbly knew he wasn't good enough yet, so he traveled to learn from those who already mastered what he needed to learn.

He surgically persisted for as long as 24 hours in many of his historic operations. It was almost a fatherly love that stirred him on—knowing the children might forever die if any of the dozens of team members made a single mistake, yet knowing the children would never truly live without taking that risk. He saw that these children born with conjoined craniums deserved liberty so he took on the responsibility of righting nature's tyranny.

What tyranny will you take on the responsibility to defeat?

Integrity + Competency = Results

Only a once-in-a-generation genius, with a humble competency, could take on that burden of an impossible procedure plus a back-to-life resurrection. To spend a year as a student preparing for each one; a humble learner with dozens of doctorates already.

Because a Dr. Carson exists somewhere, all conjoined children everywhere can hope to be set free. Hope threatens like that.

Because America exists, the hope for freedom invades children's chests everywhere.

George Washington's discipline of the army and stern resolve earned him his authority. He even once built gallows forty feet high so that he might threaten to hang two men as examples. Threats by power, after all, are nothing more than representations of a promise. Only a truly empowered entity able to enforce a threat can bestow mercy. Mercy, the sheath, requires the capable sword of authority to act. Both George Washington and Ben Carson brought peace by threat of bloodshed.

SLAMMING THE TYRANNY

Following a four-year pause to mind his business affairs after the Revolution, he was unanimously elected President of the Constitutional Convention as soon as a quorum was reached.

He was a wise counselor. Over those four months, he did not say a word in session. He let the immature patriots of Congress have their skirmishes, but in the end, they did what they knew would please Washington. They did not even need to ask him—he had already lived out a life as an example to them. His mere presence became the convention's agreement.

Washington was chosen as the United States' first President in 1789 by unanimous vote because only he could command the requisite respect across the various national and international factions. He again reluctantly accepted. In April, he was inaugurated at Federal Hall on Wall Street in Manhattan.

Many wanted Washington to remain in office in perpetuity. Even to make him king by force. But that was not his way.

Washington rose to become the sole giant of American power for the next 250 years through humility in service to we his people.

Washington chose not to seek a third term as President. Slamming the tyranny of the British crown, he proclaimed that he would not seek "unfair power as a government official."

By this lone act of humility, the most powerful Washington, who never fathered any children, became the Great Father of a people through his grace and mercy.

THE LESSON: COMMAND UNVEILS CHARACTER

England's King George III reigned for 60 years. When told Washington would step down from the presidency, he proclaimed:

"If he [steps down as ruler], he will be the greatest man in the world."

Self-proving praise from his greatest enemy is always a pointer toward great fathers. When he who tries to kill a man exalts him, we must take note. When he sentences a man to death, and then extols his innocence, those notes typically sing the highest truth. Ask Saul. Ask King George. Ask Pilate.

"Nothing that you have not given away will ever really be yours."
—C.S. LEWIS

Unlike Paris after his death in the Iliad, the newfound eternal capital city was named in Washington's honor while he still lived. Because Washington gave everything, he received it back in a manner best explained by C.S. Lewis.

Washington's successor in office nearly a century later, Abraham Lincoln, once remarked, "Nearly all men can stand adversity, but if you want to test a man's character, give him power."

Those who seek power rarely deserve it.

Command unveils character.

Men escape the darkness of tyranny by reflecting the light of Christ's freedom.

And like Washington, Jesus' refusal to become King—despite being brought into the capital city of Jerusalem in pomp and palm branches—makes Christ greater and more powerful than every king, if our enemy King George III was correct. He reflects his eternal Father, present, in a form far greater than Troy's Paris whose offspring founded the great city in France. Paris' princeship of Troy was stolen by death, while Washington willingly crucified his throne at the peak of his powerful life.

The greatest masters have always sacrificed their ambition for those they love. And they have the funny tendency to bring back to life those who the evidence guaranteed were dead: defeated armies, heart-dead children, heirless princes, your family, and yes, a Son.

*He who seeks power shall be
trounced by he who diffuses freedom.*

Grace and mercy can only arrive from a threatening force. A powerless man cannot give mercy. A weak unholy man not only cannot threaten death. But he can never offer life.

You need to stop and ask yourself,

- "Why am I threatened by powerless people I will never meet?
- Why do I lose sleep over them?
- Why do keyboard warriors take up more concern than the evil warriors trafficking child slaves?"

Your worry and concern for safety are nearly always false covers for your selfish hoarding.

*A weak man is an unholy man.
Not only because he cannot threaten death
but because he cannot offer life.*

All good fathers understand true power lies not in titles but in presence. Just ask the inmates of our prison system about a good father. Ask your own children. The answer is always the same across the range of innocence: the presence of a good father makes all the difference.

And the best Father would make an appearance to his children. Presence is the ultimate gift because you only have one of you to give.

INVERSION:
THE COMPETENT GIVE

At the end of World War II in 1945, American nuclear dominance proved absolute over Japanese forces. At that very moment, America could have ruled every country on the planet by abject fear. America's leaders knew better, looking and praying backward to Washington, Our Father.

In business, hereto, comes a critical lesson I've learned over the past twenty-five years—essentially as a professional negotiator. Be kind, quiet, and forgiving. Play the fool. Let others—especially your adversaries if you are on the same team—win the small battles. Let them believe you are no threat to them. Let them believe you think they are superior. Hand them small wins and let them see you do it. For in doing so, you allow their pride to build your enemy's gallows for you.

But remember Step 1: pick your enemies well because they are more important than your friends.

He who diffuses power freely gains supremacy. But know it is always greater to make your enemies willingly fight for you than to destroy them, in the Machiavellian and Sun Tzu sense. Coalitions are better than corpses. It's more practical to be participatory than to destroy. It's actually princely, as depicted in Machiavelli's most famous book *The Prince*.

> *To be feared while being loved is*
> *the highest form of strategic domination.*

Your most dangerous enemies are those selfish losers who never give so they have nothing left to lose. Therefore, they can never be strategically kept alive. You see them everywhere.

- The men who walk themselves to their gallows.
- The 1920's Germany the original Allies should have watched.
- The business partner who owes you more than you are worth then defaults on your partnership yet again.
- The friend who you know finds joy in your falls.

In business, war, and life:

- Victory arises through loss.
- The greater the loss, the higher the victory.
- The longer the loss, the longer the victory.
- The deepest and longest loss, the maximum conquest.
- You will not keep what you never give up freely.

Lasting mastery comes through sustained meekness. Only the strongest can afford to be lavish while they vanquish. Only a wise man will afford a sacrifice. Only he will fund his own army to defend those he loves, at risk of bankruptcy of all he has, like Washington. Only a wise man like Dr. Carson would interrupt his educated life to return as a servant-student to save a child. But we are ignorant toward competency and humility and pass it by.

Our human knowledge expands into a sea of ignorance. As our knowledge increases, so too does our awareness of our own unknowns.

And if we are wise, we will believe we don't yet know what we need. We will accept the premise that a Black Swan event is always on the horizon—yet unseen.

Like hope, these events and types of people threaten despots, disease, and downward aim.

Sometimes Black Swan events look like men of humble competency who threaten to bring a certain world-shattering hope. Ask yourself, "What would my life look like if I built true competence in something the market valued—a real trade or skill—and executed that craft with all the humility and sweat I could muster?"

- You would be purposeful in your craft and stand up tall.
- You wouldn't let people talk down to others or you'd protect them.
- You would begin to become the type of man who is emboldened to market himself and defend causes you care about.
- And that will make you more interesting to be in a friendship with, and more formidable to be at war against.

SAFETY OR MEANING.
NEVER BOTH.

My toughest negotiations always involve long-term investments. I am always negotiating the purchase or the sale of a real estate or private equity investment.

Investing is not an act of taking but of giving. Your money is given to an entrepreneur to take a risk on his success. So, wealth building is not an act of greed but of trust. But how does the wealthy man avoid becoming greedy? How does the successful man refrain from building his ego?

The solution for both the rich and the poor—in nonprofit work and investing—is precisely the same: generosity.

The rich man's generosity, when he gives anonymously, destroys his own greed by proving to himself that he neither needs the safety of that money nor does the money control him. But his gift also does something else: it serves as a salve to cure the plight of the needy. And perhaps the same selfless act serves both master and servant, President and people, rich and poor. Those who heal others may hope to be healed themselves.

To invest and to give away become the same thing if your heart is right. But you must be competent in your dealings—never lazy.

> *To invest and to give away become the same thing if your heart is right.*
> _____

Because if you are wise, you will begin to notice that the handful of people who left the world a significantly better place sowed not only their money but their very lives, into an effort more relevant than their selfish desires. And their chosen relevant work produced a harvest greater than those investing sowers could have ever imagined. Washington has never been wealthier in relevance than he is now—250 years after his death. He traded the planting of apple seeds at Mount Vernon, for the planting of his life to sprout America. Blood is the seed of freedom.

You reap what you sow. Your seed, the sweat of your brow, must be planted if you ever hope to have a harvest, or a tree to shade you. The investment funds must be handed over if you ever want a return, or even to keep up with inflation.

Uninvested talent, seeds, genius, capital, and fathers all become nothing. The work you don't do evaporates your future.

> *The work you don't do evaporates your future.*
> _____

THE LAW OF C.S. LEWIS

Remember: Washington was first a rebel before he could have become a king. And if a rebel can get his life together, there's hope for all of us who rebel against our masters by trying to keep our unworthy enemies, trinkets, and safety.

Why couldn't that kind of hope to prevail exist somewhere? And if it existed somewhere, couldn't it happen anywhere? I think here we must return to C.S. Lewis' law:

Nothing that you have not given away will ever really be yours.

We mistakenly believe that our lives are better protected and insulated in safety. But it is just past the edge of safety where life really begins. Because the edges you don't pass become the prison walls enslaving your purpose. And when you value your safety, you reject a real life. And eventually rejecting safety, you reject learning and competency.

So what is Lewis saying we should give away? Money? Okay—here's a fist full of cash and I'll be done. No.

Reality does not value tokens. It values sacrifice. And you can only sacrifice what you value, or at least you better only sacrifice something you value, as we learned in Step 4. Only what's worthy of keeping—and hoarding—is worthy of giving away.

Life begins just past the edge of safety.

So, I find that when I am most irritated and spiteful toward my family because they are taking up my time for errands when I am busy, it is because I have not been giving away my love and time to them properly.

I must freely give away love if I am to recognize the love of my family. If I pay attention and invest first, I will get back mountains more than I give. You can have safety or meaning. Never both.

You can have safety or meaning. Never both.

When I'm selfish and hoard my money when business is good, I'm cowardly seeking safety for the upcoming storms of life. I lie that I am "being a wise steward" and protector of my family, not realizing I am becoming a selfish tyrant. Tyrants take and never invest. When I see this side of me come out, I know the only proper thing to do is to give it away anonymously. If I give it away with my name attached, I convert my greed into more pride.

We first give it away THEN possess it. But are the things we give away—money, time, love, favors—the actual point of the act of possessing in Lewis' sense? What more could I give but my time, money, and love?

We first give it away THEN possess it.

Step 3 tells us that what masters us defines us. To be mastered by a master could mean different things: If I am being mentored by a financial expert, I may be willing to put my money under their control because they know more than me. Likewise, if my wife and I are attending a marriage seminar, I am putting my desires and feelings into the hands of the marriage professional as my master on that topic—but I would never give that counselor my money to invest in real estate or bitcoin. We pick and choose different masters for different objectives.

Keeping C.S. Lewis' law in mind, I ask you to think back to Step 4: only our wills can lay themselves down on the altar of sacrifice and be pleasing to the gods. Our wills and our vows are what the gods demand from us. Because they know from our highest ultimate vow, all the other agreements and covenants of our lives cascade. Therefore, the handling and investing of our love, time, and money cascades from our highest vows. Your vow determines whether or not you will give any of it.

Because in the rightly-ordered man, his highest vow was to the highest master he could find. In Step 4 I told you sacrifices looked like vows and both could bring revelation.

But what I didn't connect for you back then was this: the will you lay down as a sacrifice requires your very life. It is a living sacrifice.

Remember what a true and noble sacrifice really is. True sacrifice is an investment not an expense. Remember Alexander the Great in Jerusalem and his sacrifice: his humility to pray and kneel in front of his army to the lowly, unguarded Jews of that time. And if the most powerful man in history could humble himself in Jerusalem, perhaps we can do it there as well.

True sacrifice is an investment not an expense.

Lewis knew exactly what he meant when he said we had to give away whatever we wanted to keep. He was not mainly thinking of money, love, gifts, power, or even promises. He was talking about ourselves.

Trying to save your life is the only sure way to lose it.

- The brave men who stormed the beaches of Normandy traded their individual lives for millions of others to live in freedom.
- Alexander reordered the whole world only after sacrificing his whole world when he knelt.
- Mother Theresa of Calcutta gave her life and raised hundreds of millions to serve the poor of Calcutta, only to die destitute. Yet she lives wealthier than me now.

A proper life will be given up for the asymmetric upside of serving the highest possible master with the sole thing we have: ourselves. Only that ultimate master is worth the gamble of our infinite life in trade. A life not given away is a death. But what appears first as a trade becomes much more.

A life not given away is a death.

That true trade will revolutionize your life and the lives of others if you will believe Lewis' single true law. And live it.

Ask yourself,

- "What if I just believe this one law: to keep I must first give away? What can that hurt?
- What suffering in others can I alleviate by giving them something I think I need?
- How would I begin to think about my worth and my dignity, if I gave when I wanted to keep?"

YOUR NEXT MOVES

You can embed this law we must all recognize into your very being. But we must do it with diligence and sincerity because whatever blesses you can threaten you.

> *Whatever blesses you
> can threaten you.*

First, consider what you do have in terms of resources, skills, relationships, and ideas. Get those skills out of the computer and off the couch, and into the real world. Write them down on a sheet of paper. And write down how you can provide them for free for someone who needs you without them asking.

- Are you a mechanic? Be available to the single mothers you meet for their oil changes and repairs at no cost.
- Are you a lawyer? Offer your skills to write the wills and business plans of the poor. I assure you, if you write enough wills and business plans for free, someone will write you in.
- Can you code? Go work for free for a start-up for a year in addition to your day job. If you are good enough, you'll get equity, a board seat, or a job.

Second, remember Step 4: if you don't know what to do next, make a sacrifice. This means to make a real gift of something you desire to the master you have chosen to serve. The quality of that gift, just as Alexander discovered only after he left Jerusalem, will determine the quality of your revelation and the magnitude of what you get back. Because you will lose whatever you try to keep.

In a sense, your life is calculated by the collection of your spent moments. But don't fear. A single universally impactful moment can outweigh them all.

Third, if you have nothing, look at what others you would trade places with have and did. And do what they did, but faster and better. Because anything one man does, so can you.

- If one man can have a loving wife because he compliments her dignity, works two jobs to provide, volunteers, and does the dishes, so can you.
- If one man can spend an evening speaking with world-class leaders, so can you.
- If one woman can give her life for the poor of Calcutta, so can you.
- If one man can be healed, so can you.
- If one man can build a business that funds a thousand-man force to fight evil tyranny, so can you.
- If one messed-up man can say the awkward words to his family, "We're going to read the Bible and pray together around the dining room table every Sunday night at 7:00," so can you.
- If one man can stick a bunch of his social media quotes together into a book like this, so can you.
- If one man can put this book down, walk into the nearest cafe, and compliment every average-looking single woman he sees and stay until he gets one phone number, so can you.
- If one man can move his computer from his office into the family room so he's not tempted to look at porn, so can you.
- If one man can work 100 hours per week and still sit at family dinner around the table, so can you.
- If one man can go door-to-door for five years and face that rejection face-to-face to become invincible to rejection, so can you.
- If one man can be resurrected, so can you.

You must be all-in on life, just as a worthy man needs to be all-in for love. Because without the vulnerability to live, love, and give, we all remain savage rebels more than we remain saving men. And like Washington, you were built to reflect a father more than to remain a rebel. Like Carson, you were built to save someone other than yourself.

*You were built to save someone
other than yourself.*

And you know deep down that you cannot save anything worth keeping—a marriage, a country, or a life—without giving up your selfish desire to hoard it.

You must take a step to give up what you most wish to keep. You must give away your skills if you ever hope to have competency. You must give away your desire for power, if you ever wish to deserve it.

For what you keep dies. It's a law of life. And of power. It's the promise of George Washington, Ben Carson, Christ, and all good leaders and fathers. It's the promise of all seeds who wish to become trees to give you both shade and fruit. The promise of all investments. And the promise of all saviors who lay down their lives on a cross instead of accepting a kingly crown.

Because somehow, your best life arrives in paradox: when you act like you will live forever but take action like right now is all you will ever have. We will arrive at this in the next chapter.

You only keep what you give away.

Imagine who you could become if you took on this responsibility of giving first to create a treasure of competency to benefit the world.

TOOL: YOUR 81-YEAR LIFE

As I write this on the glass top desk in my office, I can look over to my right and see a sheet of paper with my entire life on it just beneath the glass. It's my life in months. It has helped me be more serious and have more fun, given me a new urgency, and aimed me to treasure the gifts of my past more. It's a single sheet of paper that communicates to me my entire life without a single word.

Right now, in 2024, the average life expectancy for a man is 74.8 years and 80.2 years for a woman. Many of you are living on borrowed time.

Let's assume fate or the gods or fortune, enjoy symmetry, just like I do. I like the idea of trinities because I see them everywhere: the three notes of a chord, the thirds that separate the notes, and the three chords that make up the basis for most Western music. So I'm going to give you all the chance of a little extra time. I'm going to give you 81 years to spend as you wish. A trinity of trinities times another to balance, or (3 × 3) X (3 × 3), of years.

You will remember this forever.

Download this tool for free at **RICKWALKER.COM/9STEPS**

DE-FRICTION

> *"But in some cases it is really more creditable to be carried away by an emotion, however unreasonable, which springs from a great love, than to be unmoved."*
>
> **FYODOR DOSTOYEVSKY**
> *The Brothers Karamazov*

The Lament of the Art of Painting is a captivating 16th-century engraving by Cornelis Cort and finished by Federico Zuccaro (Zuccari). This allegorical piece explores the vulnerability and nobility of artistic endeavor, showcasing intricate detail and emotive depth. The radiant woman representing Wisdom, is pointing to the gods and triumphing over Envy, who lies defeated underground in hell. Courtesy of The Metropolitan Museum of Art.

Courtesy: The Met, New York City.

View this art in full color and resolution at RickWalker.com/9steps

STEP 8

ACT LIKE YOU WILL LIVE FOREVER.

Live like there's no tomorrow.

THE SET-UP:
GO WATCH A MARATHON

WE NOW COMPLETE the chapter pair of my struggles from the first chapter. This is where the tensions of my life were resolved. The life flip. The inversion. The burning up of my beginning story as a fiery sacrifice to a real future adventure. More exciting than wearing tuxedos, GQ parties, spies, and terrorists. Where the proper vertical thinking about the internal and external factors from the other three chapter pairs in-between begin to converge. Here is the rare wisdom you and I really need to escape the gravity of our circumstances no matter how hard we try. And this wisdom glues our horizontal actions to a transcendent vertical morality, yielding a powerful launch in our advantage. You have the fuel. Here is the ignition.

Act like you will live forever, but know all you have is today. Let me tell you a story of why both are necessary.

My wife Shannon takes good care of herself. She eats well and exercises several times a week. She wants to live a healthy and long life. For a few years now, she has run most weeks. She began running half marathons four years ago in a foursome of ladies.

One Saturday morning in 2023, during a practice run she couldn't make, one of her foursome fell with a heart attack. She passed away a few weeks later, from the impact of that episode. Shannon was devastated that she was not there to be with her during those last few minutes of coherence and physical life. Shannon told me Melissa loved to live in the moment.

To live both in the moment and to live forever is the paradox of every thinking man trying to build a relevant life.

So my wife and three friends determined they would run the next year's half marathon twice—once for themselves and once for their friend. So Shannon ran her first full marathon this past February—I am so impressed by her. It is quite an inspiring feat, nearly killing a person the first time they do it.

Now, if I had not known Shannon but had seen her run that full marathon as a passerby, I could make a few conclusions about her. I could determine that she has a responsible diet, exercises regularly, and is a disciplined person.

Because I know this, I can make other conclusions: I see her run with three other friends—encouraging each other, being encouraged by their respective families, staggered along the route, sharing snacks and Gatorade, and dressed alike—I can assume she's a likable person. She has friends. And someone who has three friends who would run a marathon together is a rarity.

Our daily lives and struggles are a little like a grueling race. Shannon is sweating and struggling through the race. She's working—not because she must, but because she commits to. Any person who can drag their body over the finish line 26.2 miles later must be a determined individual. A determined individual who can run and keep others running next to them for twenty-six miles has integrity, competency, and influence.

Shannon's external fortitude is a virtue of her inner strength. The discipline and desire to do the right thing when the wrong thing keeps knocking. And each step is a knock at the door of quitting. Each stride forward is an attack on evil comfort; it's the right thing when the easy thing has no consequences. A person who can finish a marathon can be trusted.

> *Each step forward is an attack on evil comfort.*

So, people see her physical characteristics: toned muscles, runner's stride, tanned physique, and the effort pouring off her. And because they can see all those they can also begin to infer something truer about her mind and perhaps her soul.

Though my wife can run a 26-mile marathon in a day, I believe she will run a more meaningful 100-year marathon with her life. And because her physical strength is a shadow of her mental strength, I believe her fortitude is a mirror of her character in the long run.

But it's just not me there watching her run that grueling marathon. Our three daughters are holding the signs and lemon-lime Gatorade next to me. The sticks of honey for energy, and barely ripe yellow-green bananas. They see her push through—past the limits of reasonable effort. They see her do something I suspect the human body was not optimized to do. They see her integrity come forth in example.

Every little girl knows her Mom is her future if she has enough faith and effort. Shannon's present mirrors her daughters' futures. Every parent knows their kids are their mirror because the parent is the limit on their potential, for now. For you become what you see. And my daughters see Shannon.

So too, Shannon sees her three daughters screaming for her lined up along that parade line. She knows if she quits or slows they will see her give in a little. And if they see her fortitude drop with that last drop of sweat, they may be tempted to mirror her and quit at some point as well.

And she takes another painful step with a broken toe. Because her loves are watching. They need someone to mirror. Deep down, we all want someone higher than us to reflect.

Her physical effort is a result of her mental fortitude, but she continues in loving faith in their future, hoping that she will both be an example of what they could be and prove who she is now. Today is her only opportunity to act.

For we are men who have lost yesterday, only hope for tomorrow, and only possess this single step.

Today is your only opportunity to act.

THE PROBLEM: WHAT IS A STEP?

And it is the same for you in your life. You have a responsibility to yourself, family, coworkers, and friends. It is not just a whim but a fortitude you are responsible to develop. And display to others. A strength to de-corrupt yourself by killing comfort while others watch you evolve. Your loves and even random children along life's way are looking for an example. You are responsible for what they see.

A step is a single act: to give up your now for what might come.

Yes, finishing your race requires a hellish run of endurance. Your sole life must be run well and consistently. And you cannot quit on the next step. In fact, it's the next step that matters most. Because each painful step creates the momentum for the next. Heaven requires a run through hell.

Each painful step creates the momentum for the next.

Somehow, maintaining faultlessness means always taking the next step in the right direction. But how would we live a perfect life under such conditions?

If our life is like running a marathon, what kind of effort would the greatest possible life look like?

I am now almost forced to bring up Christ as the obvious next step. I told you he'd return. He always does. He's the universal perfect man of all of this, regardless of whether you are Jewish, Hindu, Egyptian, Greek, secular, or Christian. He's where you would complete your search if you were curious enough to look for the ideal example of what a man could be. He's the historical fact if you look around and study the hero's journey in all the greatest fiction of Homer and every myth.

He's the philosophical ideal when you reason through what could possibly be the maximum hope. What else would it look like? He will always exist because He always has existed. And what always exists can never be destroyed. And that undestroyable man is the hope of us all, and therefore Christ is the maximum hope. But we shake him away because he's too obvious.

If you look out with a curious-enough worldview, whether you are religious or not, you would conclude that all these things would be fulfilled in someone like Christ. I'm trying not to be preachy throughout, but I'm also just trying to make it clear that some of this, if you're going to spend years and years reading and thinking on these topics, about relevance and world-shattering change, and becoming Plato's best possible man, it would look a lot like a very specific historical person. He's the inescapable man who was always inevitable.

Beyond every other man possible to imagine, Christ commits the greatest possible action: to save us from our death with his steps. While all of humanity watches. He too once struggled on the streets of Jerusalem while His loves looked on to see if He would quit on them. He did not.

Like Christ, you also need a marathoner's fortitude, which exemplifies who you are and what you believe you could become. Others are looking to see if you will quit on them or will stay committed.

This is the next step: the belief you can move from where you are now toward who you are meant to mirror.

Your steps determine your finish.

Believe you can step away from where you are now toward who you were meant to mirror.

But you must commit violence against the evil of quitting—to give comfort a full fight. He, as the model Master to mirror, will help you. His magnificence defeats malice and redeems our night-focused eyes with His lighted endurance. Because He offers His power to those who want truth and real love.

But a conversion is not the conclusion I am arguing for. Don't write me off that quickly. I am arguing for these 9 Steps and not for any religion. I do not believe in religion. Neither did Christ who was killed by one.

To see Shannon glistening in her physical preparation, mental fortitude, and relational competency running past her girls, I glimpse each stride as each unifies all her natures and all her loves in mysterious meaning more dignified than any words she could ever speak. Her strides are holy as long as they continue. She had taken our family's love to the streets. And if anyone was paying attention, the private lessons and moments of our little family could be beheld by everyone who saw her steps.

Your striding and striving beats back the devil tempting you to slow down and give up on today's potential.

As that grieving husband watching my wife run the marathon for his, the effect of a sweet joy of remembrance took over his teary face. For though she died, she lived in a drop more than a memory that day. It was a sweetly unfolding paradox birthed in sweaty pain.

If one of us can take a holy step to defeat evil, so can you.

Evil wants you to take your time. And time is evil's tool. But how can time be beat? How can we evolve to overcome our wandering and commit to taking action today?

How do you break free to run free?

You must evolve.

HISTORICAL: EINSTEIN'S THEORIES

The 26-year-old German savant published a mostly ignored landmark paper a century ago, "On the Electrodynamics of Moving Bodies," which completed a three-century-old work known as Galileo's Theory of Relativity.

Albert Einstein girded his predecessor's work with thought experimentation to create a theory for far broader contexts. But only where the speed of light is constant.

And as Einstein knew, it must be beautiful if it is to be a high, unifying truth. So he imagined running alongside a beam of light in a lovely, perfect stride.

Truth is always beautiful.
———————

> "A theory is more impressive the greater the simplicity of its premises, the more different are the kinds of things it relates, and the more extended its range of applicability."
> ALBERT EINSTEIN

Einstein's single theory is unbelievably applied not only to mechanics and electromagnetism but also to much of physics itself. The theory also reconciled multiple scientific fields—then even back another 250 years, from Galileo to Newton—an event echoing both forward and backward in time.

He's saying theories are types of arbitrage. And the wider the arbitrage of an idea, the more impressive. So stick with me here.

So, why was Einstein's initial Special Theory of Relativity called by its modifier "special"?

Because it applies only where spacetime is flat. But natural spacetime is rarely flat because it involves gravity, heavy masses like stars, and long distances, and so it curves. His first special theory—his arbitrage of science—was limited.

Over the following decade, Einstein's General Theory of Relativity began to swallow scenarios in deep space—where gravity is so strong that even light cannot escape, such as black holes.

Einstein gifted us a greater scope—plus precision. He leaped out of Newtonian physics into special relativity and general relativity. His single mind was fixated on unifying, trusting beauty to arbitrage facts into a more valuable world.

And that's the purpose of a maximal story with maximal arbitrage: a simple formula with the greatest possible scope encompassing not only religion but philosophy, psychology, mythology, history, my false sacrifices, and all of science. For science's marathon is a search for Truth. Beauty's marathon is a search for a target at which to aim. It will ingest and arbitrage all sorts of worlds, theories, philosophies, and religions to create a more valuable story with a more beautiful end.

But how do science and steps beautify? What does that mean for you as you fight evil time and your desire to give up moving ahead today?

- Imagine what your life could be like if you went to war against the fear of wasting your life.
- Imagine what you could accomplish if you took on the responsibility of living forever.
- Imagine what sort of man you could become if you were determined to take a single step of difficulty every day for the next 30 days. 60 days. 365 days.

Would you even recognize that man?

Imagine mirroring the man who follows the strongest model of persistence, competency, and giving. What could you become?

SUB-LESSON:
IMAGINING SPACE-TIME

Let me give you an example. Einstein gave us a new perspective to prove his theory as he ran along a beam of light in his imaginative marathon-like experiments. Time, our enemy was being attacked by this genius man as he ran.

Time's ugliness and hopelessness tried to sink us, but it was flipped into a beautiful story. Like Einstein, you also will see that story if you will just change where you stand, or run, when you look for it. A little imagination never hurts either.

*"But Einstein came along and took space and time out of the realm of stationary things and put them in the realm of relativity—**giving the onlooker dominion over time and space**, because time and space are modes by which we think and **not conditions in which we live.**"*

DIMITRI MARIANOFF,
Einstein: An Intimate Study of a Great Man

Einstein devolved time from a force into a mere mode of thinking. It was almost as if Rembrandt's seascape had called Einstein's Jewish mind to join the journey into the timeless canvas where Einstein's genius was untrapped to conquer the entire dimensionality of time because a greater mind called him to take a step.

Centuries ago, a flat world was eventually cast aside for a spherical world. Suddenly Einstein entered to tell us our space-time is not flat either. He is telling us time is bent itself. We are not made to be bent by it. Specifically, time and space are "not conditions in which we live." Yet we have a hard time accepting that the time around us is no longer as undefeatable as it once was, just as we first rebelled against the idea that the world was round.

Anything that can be bent, as light bends, will eventually break. Time itself is cracking already if such a thing as mass exists somewhere.

The whole world is attracted to the Sun. It is the Sun's attraction itself that warps light and bends time.

> *Mind what attracts you,*
> *for it will bend you.*

And, of course, the beauty of the earth from the horizon of space stems from the shadow of the darkness curving to escape our sunless depths. Like that darkness in Rembrandt's stormy seascape kissed by yellow salvation.

This is a little like the love and beauty of a marathoner, or a living man, hoping to take the next step despite the pain. Hope cracks the struggle.

Mass is like hope. Any of it changes everything everywhere.

> *Mass is like hope.*
> *Any of it changes everything everywhere.*

Mass creates gravity. So if there is any mass anywhere, time will forever be in the process of breaking everywhere.

And therefore, your nemesis, time, is being defeated and is merely a false enemy trying to remove your hope through regret, indecision, and the mirror you look into each morning as you age.

What Einstein's imagination saw, as he ran along that beam of light, was what we rebelled against. But if we look with our high imagination, instead of our low intellect, we will begin to see Einstein's running unlocked a high, unifying truth that was simply beautiful. And freeing if we will listen. Like Shannon's runner's stride that won't quit because her desire to reach the finish line is pulling her in like a gravitational force. Her stepping confirms her mothering as long as our daughters are watching and imagining her as their mirror.

Looking for the facts, we miss the magic.

Looking for the beauty, we find the truth.

Since time is broken, you will live forever, or not at all.

AN ANALOGY OF THE SUN

Would you please allow me to borrow an analogy that goes a little deeper than most of us are accustomed to? If this gets a little too difficult to follow, just skip to the next section.

Recall the Chinese Yin and Yang, which are the white Yang contrasting the dark evil Yin. Remember the ancients of Egypt and their sun deities. Think of David, the Jewish King, and his songs. All these are used to refer to Jesus Christ, who is the Greek Logos and Orderer, as being like the Sun. The infinite story of his life, death, and resurrection is like the Sun's mass shaping the universe of our everyday lives. His step down into history fulfilled all these ancient philosophies. And that is one reason I can say what is coming is a universal statement about science, history, and meaning, and not a religious statement.

As the Sun draws Earth in physically, perhaps the Sun-man who stilled the seas, storms, and souls of now fourteen men, could draw in the rest of you, as a driven runner is drawn by momentum and love into his next step.

I imagine if it came to Earth, the Sun's gravitational power would be too great to shake. And I suspect it would impact us forever because if science is correct, everything natural in breaking time will be pulled out of time's chains—perhaps even us.

A ray of light will bend around a star like the Sun because it is attracted to gravity beyond itself. And more powerful than itself. And there is no star greater than the Sun in world religions or our nature: from the Jews to the Egyptians to Jung's savage Ergon peoples. And no other star we feel carries a gravitational force like our Sun.

Mind what attracts you, for it will bend you.

DEFEATED BY A STORY

Even before they see Shannon, my three daughters hope to see her running down the road, in a way that their faith in her eventual physical presence pre-impacts who they become before it happens. And as Shannon runs past our girls they see the sweat of her past miles pouring down her forehead. And that memory of her example will last their lifetimes and play a role in how they raise their own children one day.

Shannon, hope, and the Sun's physical mass are a little like Christ: any of Him at any time threatens all of time.

> *Christ's presence at any time threatens all of time.*

The arc of the Sun's shade on our earth shows beauty often comes from a curvature-like bend of the darkness contrasting the light. Perhaps our beauty also comes from our bent hearts once our lives are redeemed by the Sun as soon as we bend our knees.

As Alexander discovered, all knees must bend upon a massive enough revelation. This revelation has been shouted to us over and over by the prophets, scientists, and poets. Yet, because we still think time is flat, so is our foot. And therefore we make excuses for not running. Or leaping.

> *"I then held, and now hold, the belief that a man's first duty is to pull his own weight and to take care of those dependent upon him; and I then believed, and now believe, that the greatest privilege and greatest duty for any man is to be happily married, and that no other form of success or service, for either man or woman, can be wisely accepted as a substitute or alternative."*
>
> THEODORE ROOSEVELT

You must bend your knee to take a stride forward. To walk. To run. To truly live. To receive a master.

And here is the problem: only gods live forever, but gods do not kneel. Alexander kneeled, conquered the entire world, then died because he was only a man.

THE GREATEST DUTY OF ANY MAN

Imagine who you could become if you began to bend your knee: to kneel and to strive. Imagine how strong you would get if you could willingly submit to the right power. Reject the trifles. Stand up against those insignificant temptations you know are worthless.

You would toss aside those temptations: getting angry before thinking, throwing trash out the window when no one is around, telling your coworker what you really think of your wife to get his advice, and backing down when you know you should step up.

Emboldened, you would begin to become the type of person others want to be around. For you would be properly aligned and have your master above you and your demons below. You would be the type of person, God-forbid, people would seek out for advice because you look like you have it all in order. Order matters.

You need to consider your forever future and think:

- "What if I choose the highest possible Master to serve, and He makes all the lower false delicacies of life irrelevant?
- Would He turn my pornography, my gaming addiction, my pride, my desire to stay safe, my deceptive false courtesies, and my hopeless and loveless life into something pleasing to Him?
- Wouldn't all these corruptions controlling me now, then fall away back into their proper place under His leadership, as the lower vows cascade from my primary vow?
- Do I even have a primary vow, or has one been assigned to me?"

And if all this happened, you would indeed begin to act with the responsibility of someone who would live forever.

- You would take care of your neighbors when they come to you for advice.
- You would bend down and take that lost puppy into your home when you were rushing to get somewhere.
- You would take your time to help others but stay up late to make sure your daily step into your future still happened.

This is taking responsibility for your entire world.

Then, you would deserve the respect because you took on the responsibility of moving forward every damn day. You would have your eyes set on living forever. You'd help people see past their ideas of futility and into a truer life of growth and prosperity. Helping others instead of pitying yourself is to become the type of real man who gives away instead of takes. And that will remake any man, no matter how worthless you think you are. No matter how worthy you think you are. Dirty as you are.

People you know will start to think you are able to do important things. Even you.

TODAYS MAKE TOMORROWS

Like the marathoner, you are also at war with comfort in the present and against time's clock. You think you will live forever like the gods, but you refuse to live your life as such. So you give up. Thinking anything worth doing should be easier than what you are experiencing, you falsely assume comfort is right. Comfort is the evil squandering your potential to take the next step.

Kneeling is hard on the knees, but joyful to the soul.

Comfort is the evil squandering your potential.

Time constantly offers you a false way out of your discomfort. Instead you need to step forward toward the master you are meant to mirror.

The wise marathoner knows the long battle is against age. Against the wear and tear of the joints and ligaments. So they will work every day in and out of season on their nutrition, stretching, and conditioning because they understand today is all they have to work with.

And if today is all you have, then your tomorrows are the results of your todays.

You are a soul more than you are a body, according to Lewis. And that means you will live forever—in splendid work or devastating comfort. Yes, the Bible's promise of forever in heaven is work, not clouds and harps. And it's this audition you call life that determines your responsibility forever.

You are a soul more than you are a body.

It is your soul part that lives forever like the gods, but a body that allows the kneeling. And in the end, it's the kneeling that allows them both to live forever. A magical union bearing a promise.

It's the temporal steps you take daily now which will determine your forever. This makes all your steps not only everlasting, but perhaps even holy.

When you choose comfort today, delaying that next painful step you ought to take, you choose your defeat by hell. Workless torture is what every day in eternal hell actually is. If you do nothing to move forward today, you bring hell into your now. And make your forever more difficult.

Choose difficult and honest work.

Evict evil sloth.

There are little eyes watching you in your home, on the streets, in the chat rooms, and in the office. And you will be held responsible for the hell you cause them to see. Since we mirror what we see, it is your fault what they become. Own it.

You are held responsible for what I see.

Either you are advancing toward heaven. Or hell. There are no sideways steps.

But where do I get the idea that work matters? That power comes, and time is futile? And where is this evolution I mentioned at the beginning of this chapter?

SUPPOSITION:
THE NEXT EVOLUTION OF MEN

The first great evolution of physics, from Newton to Einstein took 250 years. There's been no unifying theory of physics since. But Einstein's single-mind revolution from special to general only took a decade. And nothing since for a century.

We now await the next evolution of mankind; the next brilliant mind to arrive to notice it. Could it take two or three more great minds another 500 years to discover that unifying framework? No. I am certainly not that mind. I am merely passing on a message I once heard.

Time is dying, but it remains destructive.

What do we need for the next great discovery to save us from time? And once saved from time, what could mankind become?

Here we need an Einsteinian revelation—no a revolution—to understand how the next great leap could happen to save humanity from dying, but savage time.

> *"The future is not a gift—it is an achievement."*
> ALBERT EINSTEIN

If we want to know something, to experience a real revelation, we return to Alexander the Great and Step 4: a revelation requires a sacrifice—of pride, will, and even those false likes which we call love. Those little facts we confuse with the truth. Those tired knees we refuse to break into a full kneel.

And even more so, we must sacrifice our desires for Christ's oughts. We must trade what-is for what-might-be. And that is how the next great evolution of mankind will begin to occur on the horizon, as the light first begins to form an arc out of the darkness of space as the Sun strikes the edge of our world.

> *We must trade what-is*
> *for what-might-be.*

Time may be breaking, but it still impacts us unless we evolve into the type of people who are not impacted by what time causes: guilt, grief, regret, and death. Because if what we need is an evolution that will save us from time's effects, like death, then we need an unknown beautiful revelation.

And I suspect it would arise from the unsuspected ordinary of Rembrandt, dinner tables, and first appear like immature college infatuation. Perhaps even as immature as a thirteen-year-old girl named Mary, holding her newborn just outside the gates of Jerusalem.

Isn't it odd that this Westerner keeps talking about a random Middle Eastern city and the Jews?

STEPPING INTO
YOUR EVOLUTION

And if all todays are eternal and time is broken, that means a revolution has already occurred—some rebels just have not accepted it yet.

But we must take that first step regardless.

And that first act or step, if made in the right direction and for the right purpose, can redeem not only all your todays but also all your yesterdays and tomorrows.

A single moment can do this.

Since a single step can be holy, you can baptize today.

Shannon's single marathon stride, which is her protest against evil comfort, is not only helping her, but it also is a flash of yellow glory enlivening the lives of our little girls as they watch her as a mirror of who they can become. They trade their what-is for what might-be because of her step.

- What if a single God-man takes just one holy step on our earth for the highest purpose: to redeem the least deserving rebels who had already quit trying?
- Could that infinite mass of meaning greater than the Sun draw more than just some nice feelings about a nice man into itself?
- Could the infinite meaning and love brought into time have any effect on us?
- Would that effect appear as an evolution, bending our wills and desires around His step's massive gravity?

And yes, I speak of the single stooping down of God Himself into time. Could that infinite imbalance ever be rectified?

THE THESIS:
THE IMBALANCE REBALANCED

And when you act like you are going to live forever, you begin to take on responsibility of the eternity which your soul already suspects it has. And you begin to defeat the narrow-mindedness your weak will and digitally-trained mind falsely hope is true.

Every step matters. Steps and todays are all you have. What would your future look like if you asked yourself:

- "What would I do if I knew I had an infinite amount of help and an infinite amount of time?
- What could I accomplish if I just did something every day believing that?
- What would others think of me if I became the sort of person who could be trusted to be wise—acting now while thinking forever?
- What sort of beauty could I see in my little life if I really believed what the science and the love I read about told me about?"

Your greatest revenge on evil time is your living forever despite it. Christ's greatest revenge on evil was his invading step as a bastard baby, infinite and vulnerable. He is not interested in fulfilling the mediocre hype of fake stories we'd invent.

Your greatest revenge on evil time is your living forever despite it.

And perhaps that next infinite step into our world to give it that balance would be inside of you. It would give you the unshakable confidence to try, fail, and dust yourself off again, knowing you have both infinite power and infinite time if you just keep moving forward down the road. Moving forward as if drawn in by something greater and weightier than yourself.

For many, to be drawn in by Christ is the real purpose of life's roads. The adventure is in the stepping when you know you don't have the power or the right. Yet you step regardless.

And if any infinite story strikes your finite heart, your heart must be made infinite and eternal to bear it.

BENT KNEES
REMAKE BENT HEARTS

Or we can use another analogy.

It's almost as if we always admired Him as a nice little piece of unthreatening artwork of hills hanging above the hearth of a summer cottage.

But the safe painting is now seen as a mountainscape surrounding us. Invading hearts like that single Christmas step. The mountains of our unseen ordinary reality step through the glass frame, crashing our attention. A higher dimension wishing to incorporate a lower.

We shall see, but will it be soon enough?

Will it be before we waste our only life thinking too small and playing too safe?

So I believe the entire world of real men and women must be resurrected in order to true-up the imbalance by this one appearance of a divine baby in Jerusalem who ended up walking as a man with a cross crashing toward a finish line. But that is not all.

Even more, when I sometimes read histories those people are promised to be made perfect in their hope—a real hope that threatens because He has already invaded once. As certainly as time is promised defeat because it once heard a drop of mass already exists somewhere.

And what His invasion left behind were books written about his nature—an example of how to live, love, and fight. And that example was itself the infinite mass that draws us in as real men and women who stepped past the lovely little painting with our duster in hand, thinking we were the ones doing the cleaning.

And as us mirroring steppers are drawn in by the infinite weightiness of Christ's nature, we absorb as paints on a canvas the next evolution of mankind with each of our steps in His direction. And our steps toward Him are always away from comfort and mediocrity. And hell. And into truth.

And our steps toward Him look a little like His upscaling brushstrokes over our mistakes. We were the ones being cleaned-up all along.

All this is offered to you despite the religions and our false pride polluting the grandeur of the mountains surrounding us already. The religions never noticed the eternal mountainscape marching in our direction, bursting the protection of our imprisoning glass walls all along. The mountains are themselves avalanching onto humanity through each great book, hero's story, failure, dinner table, and hopeful analogy.

They threaten because they are, as Christ is, on the move. And quite dangerous.

But what the hell does all that mean for you?

THEORY:
CHRIST'S STORY AS REFLECTION

We wrap ourselves in the hope of one day discovering a story of someone greater taking up our cause and running a marathon we could never run, like Shannon once did when she ran that marathon for her departed friend. You need:

- To carry and be carried along.
- Someone to protect and care for.
- Someone to defend and be defended.
- Someone to sacrifice for and to learn to love.
- Someone to dredge up the abscess of your soul to discover that remaining drop of courage I know is still there.

Think of your future self: "What could I learn if I were to take responsibility for the defense and care of one other person? What could I learn about love if I first love someone before they love me? What could I earn and give up again if I were to take the risk of investing into bettering my writing, speaking, and thinking skills on that off-chance I could be asked to lead some little effort just one time in my life, even if I had been set back a hundred times? What could I learn by blending a drop of courage into a cup of competence?"

- You'd be the type of person others would enjoy being around. Including yourself.
- You'd be that person everyone at the school and chat room depended on to take on impossible conversations.
- You'd take that newfound courage and competency and serve one other person first. Then many other people. Because you knew you could be trusted.
- You might fall down, but you know you'll get back up.

And knowing you will rise back up is more than everything.

Christ also came to be our example on the streets of Jerusalem to mirror, to paint His nature onto our nature. The only way to make His steps greater would be for His single act to unify both the triumph of the greatest good imaginable and the unsurpassed defeat of the greatest evil thinkable in the greatest arbitrage possible. He took His death and traded it up for our life.

I am speaking here not about religion or conversion, but about history, philosophy, symbolism, and purpose, which guide the 9 Steps as they guide every Judeo-Christian nation's morality.

Christ's story is not only the fulfillment of the wishes of the true philosophies and false religions—but the fulfillment of real history. All of that in one God-man whose enemies call his archetypes the Sun, Krishna, Logos, and Messiah. Except He refused to become king.

Then that dimension-uplifting, domain-unifying man steps forward into the lives of all humanity lined up along that dirt road in a number of ways: in Jerusalem's history, reading of the story, or hearing the eyewitness accounts passed down through the generations. Or perhaps reading the prophecies of Isaiah, David, Plato, and Daniel centuries before He ever stepped through those gates like Alexander to make a sacrifice.

Remember when told Washington would step down from the presidency, England's King George III proclaimed: he will be the greatest man in the world.

Man's purpose is to live as He lived and do what He taught: To love one another as He loved. To give up our wants, needs, and desires—even our life—for the weak on the streets around us who don't deserve anything. And to do it with a kind of Carsonesque vulnerability.

And somehow—in some way I don't understand—this is how He gets His power into those who want to become real men more than they want to remain rebels.

Just as once my girls lined up to see Shannon on a holy road in Houston somehow built my daughters. They lined up to see what they could become by seeing Shannon, their co-creator. And seeing they now hope to one day become as she is already. And are stepping toward her example.

It's a little like that. Christ mirrors Himself onto you and me as well, if we will pay attention to His story. But we have the focus of a bumblebee.

The lines on the pages of the greatest book in history shout the same lines and loves to us all: courage, bravery, love, a cross. And only then: joy and perhaps a crown.

Despite your deceit and dark demise, Christ will shine a little light in your direction to see if you'll look back at Him. That's how He caught me. All great hunters wish to catch the reflection of a gazing eye in the wild darkness.

YOUR NEXT MOVES

Now allow me to set some actionable steps you also can take if you want to live like an evolved man. If you are determined to follow this rule and act like you will live forever. Because you will. Because you are a soul more than you are a body.

You need your soul to live and your body to kneel to get the forever part of the promise. You, I, and Alexander the Great are the same deep down.

First, today is all you have. Whatever you do, leave tonight better off than you found it this morning. Today is the only stepping stone toward your forever.

Make today the servant of your tomorrow.

Do the most difficult and lasting thing right away each morning, and do nothing else until that is done. Don't eat. Don't pick up the next interruption. Don't open another screen.

> *Make today the servant*
> *of your tomorrow.*

If you have to choose between work which is urgent and something which is important, ignore the urgent. Urgent work is rarely important.

Anything that can be taken away never really belonged to you.

Likewise, choose the action with the longest positive upside and reject the action that can disappear tomorrow. Do not ignore the lesser for the greater, for that's a great sin.

> *Anything that can be taken away*
> *never really belonged to you.*

Consume blogs over tweets, because blogs are tougher to read and last longer. And books over blogs. Choose to read an older book over a newer book because it has lasted longer.

And perhaps a bit of that greatest book's millennial longevity will rub off onto you.

Second, honor the dead. If you listen to the perspectives of current influencers and colleagues without considering the views of the past thinkers, you miss out. In fact, you rob the dead of their vote. Great ideas demand a vote. And those whose ideas have stood across time, deserve a greater weighting than the narrow optics of the men who are recent.

Lastly, keep taking steps every day. If an action is longer-term and holy, it sanctifies all the other imperfect thoughts and desires of your day as well.

> *One step can sanctify all the imperfect thoughts*
> *and desires of your past.*

And a holy day is an eternal day, because great work is rewarded eternally. Poor and directionless work creates a hell in both your now and forever.

A consistent step on a day you don't feel like it makes you stronger than a day when your steps are easy. Do one hard thing every day. And if you need a place to begin:

- Leave your house by 5:00 AM and do not return until 5:00 PM.
- Go sit in a cafe with a book, buy 10 strangers' lattes, and build some relationships.
- Just walk into the gym and don't leave for an hour.
- And whatever you do, keep all your devices anywhere other than in the room where you sleep. Phones destroy more marriages, virginities, and attentions than you will ever know.

Go get some life. Go give some life as well.

Recall Step 7: you lose what you try to keep. In the Biblical sense, it comes across as you only reap what you first plant.

If you plant worthless work, you reap worthless results. If you never struggle to help others, anything anyone does for you will become futile.

Because all you have is today. And all you have is you with the promise of an infinite power to help you if you choose the right Master.

And your comfortable and step-less days are certainly destructive. That's how losers are made—not by losing but by rarely trying. Holy gifts burn up in the hands of a man with the hellish pursuit of ease. But you can begin trying and trusting, without excuses, and turn that around in the next 30 days.

> *Holy gifts burn up in the hands*
> *of a man with the hellish pursuit of ease.*

The Catholics, which I am not, say we shall partake of the maximal story possible, as we eat bread, fruits, and drink grape juice after a marathon week. The Hindus also rejoice in the light of the Diwali feast. Nourishing our lowly depleted bodies, while filling our divine souls with gratitude. This is what a great story would feed us like. I suspect they have that right because a story is just a collection of steps taken to advance our souls over a bunch of todays.

And perhaps it is possible that accepting the greatest story imaginable as truth is the mechanism by which the next great evolution of mankind—to usurp death and guilt—happens to work. And perhaps that's what you need: an evolution. I did.

For if someone had run for the highest possible purpose, they must've carried others. Maybe a billion. No one can technically do anything better than this: to give life to the dead.

Running and struggling over a string of todays, your tears and sweat mix into a sop of joy. But only if that kind of highest purpose is there in your todays. For all runners know once they feel their energy sapped, a drop of yellow honey will bring them renewal. And storms bring out the sun.

Struggles become joy if your step is in the right direction.

I've heard bloody crosses might even become golden crowns. I bet you witness it everywhere. But society tells you to ignore it.

- The birth of every child out of a dark womb.
- The rise of every wheat seed sowed and reaped for food out of the dark soil.
- The landed bird rushes to take flight yet again.
- A son sees his Dad protect his Mom.
- A hundred men lavishly demand justice on evil.
- A hundred tears lavishly demand justice on death.

The effort you give today determines your forever. What you plant now will be verified by the future of what you ever get. So get moving today. Expect discomfort and trial. Expect waning energy. Those are cues for you to raise your fist and fight on.

The effort you give today determines your forever.

Sowing shall be reaping. In your life and in the entire cosmos. That is the promise offered if there is another great evolution of man.

The mirroring of the supranatural power onto you is offered to you. The Master Painter's brush is already in one hand, and all His dark contrasts and light yellows sit in the Painter's palette in the other. And the same drop of yellow threatens all your stormy yesterdays with the hope of a golden crown tomorrow. He may just use all His paints on you because you're worth His attention. And though you wish to be two-dimensional, He's building up colorfully deep layers you cannot see. He is building up a real boy.

I think He uses the yellows most when you notice the ordinary around you: those unmanufacturable miracles in your dreams, the guilt, math, DNA, self-healing tumors.

Expect the magic. And the evolution.

A REAL GIRL'S MORE THAN A FAKE FATHER

A few days after Shannon's marathon, my 13-year-old middle daughter Lily-Kate, took to the lacrosse fields. Finding her team down zero to six, the loss seemed apparent. Even the parents gave up on their own kids. But not Lily-Kate. From 99 yards away I could hear her mimic the encouragements she heard from Shannon toward her friends in that marathon.

My daughter, beyond all hope and all reason, roused her teammates to call forth the undiscovered fortitude to take a stand on defense. And to convert that defensive stand into an offensive invasion. She called forth the promise that not only did she believe in her teammates, but that she expected them to rise up in that moment. You see, it's okay to borrow a greater person's faith in you. Even a little girl.

And over the next twenty minutes, I watched this mini-mirror of Shannon storm the other team's goals and dash their hopes. Because a drop of Lily-Kate's hope had stepped onto the field to resurrect the spirits of her low-aimed teammates. And as Lily-Kate scored the next goal I saw her glance over to the sidelines at her little sister, Rosie, to make sure she was watching her big sister's beautiful violence threaten certain defeat. You become what you see.

Lily-Kate won the game and earned the respect of all those fake fathers who had given up on their own kids. Never give up on a real girl who has more faith than you. Never forget the power of a parent's example rippling through the entire family. Inspiration reflects and refracts out to others in wild lavishness.

Remember the wisdom of the arts when you take action each day so that Christ's maximal life would reflect back into you: live as a vulnerable man willing to die so that hope-giving power may peek through the clouds of others.

The oboe: the most vulnerable of all the instruments.
The swan: the most vulnerable of all the animals.
The dancer: the most vulnerable of all the beauties.
My little girl: the destroyer of defeat.

None surpassed in grace. None more at risk of tragedy. We are all as the en pointe ballerina. We are all the certain loser on the field calling out for others to rise up. Exposed. Alone. Afraid. Demanding vindication.

Imagine your one swift stride today can defeat the badness of all your yesterdays ruling your life right now. I believe one foot-strike in history already has. And if one of us has done it, so can you.

Keep moving. And move with violent beauty.

The stage is now yours.

Take the field like you only have today. Take steps and risks based on a 5,000-year framework instead of a 5-minute feeling. You'll become the type of man who can be trusted. Who people come to when they are in trouble. Who likes what he sees in a mirror because he's dirty from the real work of a real life of cleaning himself up on the inside.

Clean your life up because you're going to live forever. And forevers are never stagnant, they always end in heavens or hells. There are no sideways steps.

In our final Step you will discover how you can unleash the truth and beauty in your work and life.

Act like you will live forever. Because you will.

And shoulder that load. Because you can.

CONCLUSION

"Between stimulus and response there is a space. In that space is our power to choose our response. In our response lies our growth and our freedom."
VIKTOR E. FRANKL

Allegory of Government: Wisdom Defeating Discord by Jacob de Wit is an 18th-century painting at The Met symbolizing the triumph of wisdom over chaos and discord. The central figure, representing Wisdom, is often depicted in serene yet commanding form, subduing figures symbolizing discord, such as quarrelsome or disheveled characters. Surrounding elements include symbols of governance, such as books, olive branches, or celestial motifs, emphasizing the ideals of enlightenment, justice, and order. The piece reflects de Wit's masterful use of light and allegory to convey moral and political themes. Government as a group of men.

Courtesy: The Met, New York City.

View this art in full color and resolution at RickWalker.com/9steps

STEP 9

SEEK BEAUTY AND YOU MAY FIND TRUTH.

If you don't know what to do, choose the option that would create the most unbelievably beautiful story for you to tell your grandkids one day. Your steps make your stories, and your stories make your life.

THE SET-UP: SELFISH COLLEGE SEX

SEEK SEX FIRST, and you will only find lust. Seek facts only, and you will only find rote logic. But build a beautiful story, and you will find truth and love. And with them, power thrown in.

As we conclude, I draw your attention back to where we began. The only way to know the true is to reject the false. The only way to love is to hate that which is not loving. Love is the glue which binds all 9 Steps. Let me show you.

Do you remember that couple who met seated in a college classroom? You know that boy and girl who started dating and almost immediately fell in love? I certainly do. I saw it a thousand times: they quickly moved from the first to daily dates. And to do that, they had to abandon their other friendships and commitments with us. Maybe this was you and your spouse?

The same annoying couple traveled home together on the holiday breaks to spend time with the other's family. They spent every possible waking second together. They were in love, after all.

But that kind of love looked more like infatuation to us outsiders who were left behind. Maybe we assumed it was just selfish college sex. But the selfish relationship part, without the sex, required the rejection of those outside to embrace that potential love they hoped would be THE one.

Those students would never know if it were true love without their rejection of all of us on the exterior to their infatuation.

This new relationship had to be tested by their sacrifice of those old friendships they valued but ultimately knew would never become the single love of their lives.

> *Love is just as much choosing who to embrace*
> *as it is picking those false likes to reject.*

———

The ancient Chinese philosopher, Lao Tzu, advised us on this 2,500 years ago:

> *"I must give up what I am in order to
> become that which I might be."*

Lao Tzu tells us that all life is about giving up our lesser likes for the higher loves. Imagine what that means for us and the loathsome trinkets of cunning and passive aggression we submit to.

Think about your future and decide:

- "I'm going to give up one activity today which would keep me down tomorrow.
- I'm committed to becoming the best version of myself others can depend on. Perhaps even someone I can admire.
- That requires me to give up worthless daily activities and embrace what I know my future self needs to become.
- I will act as if I am already on my way to my future self, so I will practice courage and develop competency with all the worthless time I am freeing up now.
- I will say no to the worthless things.
- For every one thing I will commit to doing, I will commit to stop doing another two."

And now bold, unburdened a little, and empowered, you can take the next step toward stopping the single mediocre thing you do the most, and replacing it with the next best thing you should do. And you take the next step toward your future ideal self.

Becoming yourself, just as the infatuated friend-leaving couple knew, is just as much about rejecting as it is embracing.

*Your past will be sacrificed
to see your future.*

Time will fatefully see to it. When that couple who rejected your friendship in college eventually married, you had a bit of relief. As the marriage continued, you likely began to lose touch with them. The couple's love had been consummated—not merely sexually or legally but also in reality. But not yet consummated to its fullest.

You see, when two lovers love each other the love is such that it is singularly focused on the other person. It realizes a bit of reflectivity and reciprocity is at play. And with reciprocity, we begin to evaluate motives. When someone can reciprocate, should reciprocate, our motives become warped quite quickly because there is an unspoken benefit to love.

Eventually, that college couple, if they are rightly aligned and after a few years of being in this singular love, decide to start a family by birth or adoption. Shannon and I did.

The wife secretly worries that the husband won't love her as much after the natural course of carrying a new life takes effect on her body. The husband worries the same, while also concerned about providing; the depravity of man's own selfish heart.

When the baby comes, it is a moment of joy. The mother extracts eternal joy from unbearing pain. The father steps into a supporting secondary role for a time. Such profound moments of joy can be found in a single breath of a child, redeeming the pain of the mother and the demotion of the father.

Love of the child takes center stage in the heart and the home. Conversations that had been focused on themselves now turn to the child. Saving and investing that had been focused on their retirement safety now turn to the child's benefit. Sleep schedules are thrown out. Work quality and career achievement are overthrown for a moment. Lavish parties with the future leaders of the world no longer dazzle.

This is all more right than before. Every loving parent knows it. It is a higher love than before. Higher loves often mean harder lives. But why?

Higher loves often mean harder lives.

Cataclysmically the motives shift over the coming days: as love takes root in the third person, the child, love expands to encompass more than before. The love of the husband and the wife must be protected while temporarily being set aside in a certain sense. The love between the mother and the child must be the controlling relationship because the bond of unexplainable charity takes root in attention.

Right worship, which is called wonder, is the outflow of proper attention.

Right worship, which is called wonder,
is the outflow of proper attention.

The attention between the father and the child gives the man a reason to grow in his nature as a protector and hero, thus developing the man's purpose and work more deeply and richly. The mothers who can do both become immortal saints.

I suppose we may have been that infatuated college couple at first. We have an amazing marriage which got to this level only after we had our girls, not before. But something even more incredible arises to overshadow the rising family dynamic which I see in all three of my daughters: Rosie, Lily-Kate, and Emerson. These four girls are my very life. I would happily kill a million savages to save one of them from harm. Wasn't that an outlandish thing for me to tell you? But it is true. Remember the first chapter when I told you about the evil beheader? You need a story worth telling your grandkids one day.

You must handle both evil and true love in lavish fashion.

Yes, DVD-sending beheaders must themselves be beheaded. I was told a hundred men were dispatched against those murderers of our one man. Because you don't send one bullet when you can send a hundred. You don't kill one savage when a million threaten. You must kill all threats to those who are in your charge to protect: addictive devices, bad food, gossipy friendships, threatening theology, and your own sensual addictions.

Lavishness is always right when dealing with evil.

And writing of love.

Imagine yourself in a true and deep love. Committed. Unreasonable. And after giving up your wants for their needs something happens in you. When you give away your love you grow and become worthy of being loved as a man. But you never realize that before. Only after.

Disproportionate love coupled with a disdain for wrong is how all men are delivered from remaining school boys.

True love is unreasonable.

THE PROBLEM:
WHERE TO BEGIN?

Time drains your hopes and fills up your fears until you overbrim with insignificance.

Fearing, you reject any appearance of vulnerability. You are unable to love or be loved properly. So you invite insignificance and hopelessness deeper and lose the power offered in vulnerability—hoping pity will come your pathetic way. How do you stop it?

Remember Step 6: you must embrace the unknown to really live. It's the adventure and story you are meant for, not the delay, safety, and easy-to-hit targets everyone else is aiming for. So you must desire something beyond yourself to run toward. A higher master to instruct all the other promises you want to make.

And doing this, you will begin to hate your meandering comfort. I did. Your old comfortable life is burned up with excuses, which you call reasons. Mine did.

Your excuses are rarely good reasons.

Stop standing around and take a step. But to where?

Your life, a series of steps, should be a story people want to hear. No one wants to hear about delays, safety, and comfort. No one will give a damn to hear anything about you unless you heightened a love or defeated an evil.

Do your excuses aim at and hit mediocrity? Mine still do. Yet even when we hate them, we continue to return to them. For a time. What we need isn't money, fame, power, to be loved, or a purpose. Or excuses. We need to see the 9 Steps, Christ, and perhaps take a step toward the life of the fully evolved man only He offers you through action. And rejecting what is not true.

But there's a long road ahead, so let me show you where I began. Since we are so much alike when we take away the experiences and failures, I bet we'll arrive at the same place just as we began from the same one.

Think about your future and ask yourself,

- "What would my life be like if I replaced screens after 5:00 PM to only read books over 500 years old?
- What would my family be like if we ate dinner around the same table most nights without our devices and asked each other honest questions?
- Would the initial awkwardness of both the books and dinners be worth the growth of my family and myself a year from now?"

Now emboldened, as I was, you will take on those grand adventures worthy of telling over the dinner tables of your own kids and grandkids one day. Your competency and courage will empower you to be interesting enough for others to care about. And, I suspect, even to believe in.

Imagine you can get that kind of adventurous life of loving and risking. Imagine you are willing to take a risk—a smart risk with a disproportionate upside. What kind of growth could you continue to see within you and in those you have called into your life? Is there a way to see this clearer? Is there a way to know how love grows stronger, more than selfish college sex and infatuation? Yes.

And if what is beautiful is always right, then you should look for beauty if you hope to ever find right truth. Righting is the verb of what Truth Himself does to those who want to see Him. And maybe wanting your life to be righted into a beautiful story is enough. And perhaps you just wandered yourself into the beauty which offers to lead you there.

If you just wanted it with your whole life, and then lived like this higher life is real, could that work? I believe it just might if you trust these 9 Steps. And I believe your shame and guilt would be banished forever in beauty's coup against evil.

Let me show you how to get magic inside you.

WHAT IS THE MAXIMAL LOVE?

When my wife and I had our youngest daughter, I fell in love immediately. Rosie is magical. She gave and still gives me the desire to be her hero, whether she wants one or not in her teenage years.

But I began to notice something that the Parisian monk, Richard of Saint Victor, also noticed as he philosophized about the same maximal type of love in the Blessed Trinity. I began to see my wife Shannon mirrored in our daughter Rosie. I loved that. Rosie's delicate eyes searching for mine to see if I was paying attention. Holding back her smile while I accelerate my goofiness to see if she will break into a laugh. She's strong just like her Mom.

Shannon noticed that Rosie began to pick up some of my mannerisms. Shannon loved that. Sometimes she hates it, like my love for Freddy's frozen custard with strawberries and my particularities, but mostly loves it. I think.

Shannon and I loved each other deeply before. But now there's this daughter who we love as well. And, somehow, when I look at Rosie, I love her Mom even more. And when her Mom looks at Rosie, she sees me and feels my love through little things like the imputed mannerisms and our shared love for Freddy's custard, strawberries, and hard work.

My love for Shannon is reflected in Rosie. Rosie's love for me is reflected in Shannon. I can look at Shannon and love Shannon, and somehow my love for Shannon as my wife is also loving my three daughters. My loving of my daughters is also loving my wife. Shannon's care for my daughters is her loving and respecting me while I am at work. My daughters' respect and love for their Mom is their loving and honoring me.

A child is a magical musical round: returning what they see from us back to us in a thousand mirroring ways.

So you see what has happened? The lesser likes of the infatuated college lovers has now turned into something greater. Something reflective—once merely direct, between two dimensions—is now also indirectly multidimensional. And in this higher love of the third person, I began to see the highest possible type of love flourish. The seed we planted became a living rose. And in this love of my daughter, I began to see the highest possible type of love flourish in my home.

I saw the emergence of sharable love. I've not fallen in false love of television reality shows—I've been plunged into a lavish life of truth that a sharable love is the highest form of life. You see, like the Sun, any weighty love must draw a third person into its orbit to endure as true and high and bright love.

A sharable love is the highest form of life.

Others must be able to warm themselves by the fire of the charitable light of the two. This is the best kind of life. This is why the Trinity, of the Father, Christ the Son, and Holy Spirit, has the triple-person maximal love needed to evict the coldness of our hearts by their blazing and massive truth.

The poet Virgil, who died in 15 BC, is asked about this in Dante's Commedia (Purgatorio, Canto XV):

> *"How it can be a good thing, or a just thing, that the sun (a good symbolizing grace and love) is distributed among a greater number of possessors and that makes them richer than if it were only possessed by a few?"*

He answers his own question:

> *"Because thou still settest thy mind on earthly things thou gatherest darkness from the very light. That infinite and unspeakable good which is there above speeds to love as a sunbeam comes to a bright body....the more charity (love) extends... to more souls that are enamored there above the more there are to be rightly loved and* **the more love there is and like a mirror the one returns it to the other.**"

He says infinite love spreads to all souls like a mirror. Just as a master painter paints a man more richly the longer he sits still to be painted.

That which is eternal collides with that which is material, amalgamating us into a transcendent revolution of a higher love which makes us braver and bolder. It gives an ordinary man with an ordinary family the maximal love of the Trinity which maximizes the life of those who look to Christ as their sole Master.

I was plunged into seeing. And seeing gives rise to a revelation toward evolution. And that revelation of the evolution now being offered you is true. And that truth is beautiful if you permit it to take root within you. And evolution may seem like a mirror.

This engraving, titled *Charity Seated Nursing an Infant, Another Sleeping on Her Lap and a Third Talking to Her*, is a masterful work attributed to a follower of Guido Reni, an eminent Baroque artist. Held by The Metropolitan Museum of Art, it depicts allegory of Charity, a personification of unconditional love, nurturing three children. The infant symbolizes innocence, the sleeping child peace, and the speaking child wisdom shared through love.

Courtesy: The Met, New York City.

View this art in full color and resolution at RickWalker.com/9steps

INVERSION:
FALSE CONTENTMENT

Seek beauty and you may find truth. Seek love and you may find loveliness. But seek power first, and you will lose everything in the end.

And here I am speaking with you—a vulnerable father who turned his poverty and weakness into building organizations, employing thousands of people, and creating millions of dollars in wealth for many. Like Alexander, I've wandered around, destroyed plenty of people, and had a taste of everything I thought I wanted. And the only reason I ever escaped was because I rejected the false experiences I had been wandering in search of in campaigns, nonprofit work, and trying to force my way.

Many of you think you want a life of fame and connections and power. So let me begin by telling you what power is NOT based on my life experiences.

- Two United States Presidents have bought me seated dinners. And too many U.S. Senators and U.S. Congressmen to count.
- I've sat with an Asian billionaire in an exclusive restaurant that no one else can access in Las Vegas. Three of us—the Billionaire, myself, and his translator—feasted on a ten-course meal, which he insisted each bite be entirely covered in gold, served by a team of seven alone in that restaurant. Following the glowing leaf dates for dessert, I was offered cases of any of the most expensive wines in the world I wished to be sent back to my home as a parting gift.
- Seated on gold-plated thrones, nibbling delicacies on 300-year-old golden china, Princess Diana's personal chef and her personal butler served ten of us. And a line of butlers stood to the side.
- Lounged on a couch of pure silver over post-dinner dessert and coffee in a business partner's living room.
- A boxed meal with eight friends on a luxury private jet outfitted to seat a hundred passengers on the way to a boy's weekend.
- Countless times seated with billionaires and the world's power-wielders.
- Meals with the Secret Service guarding my house and dinner table because of who came over.

But I have one favorite dinner ever. None of these experiences could ever match it. This was a seated dinner with far truer Power. Because a beautiful story, bricked by dusty books and art, paved the path which brought me there.

This narrow path will look average and ordinary at first. But remember, the Black Swan events that invade our world threaten to evolve our vulnerable ordinary into a mind-shattering outlier in a single unguessable moment.

SOMETIMES WANDERING IS PRAYER

From where I sat in 2021, I saw that my prideful desires were aimed low with amazing dinners, business success, and dream experiences. I wanted what I saw in the private jet, golden dishes, servants wearing tuxedos, and powerful men. Like Alexander, we all know deep down even the whole world is not enough for any of us. Yet we wander around for it anyway.

I needed a revelation. Do you? I trust that by showing you how my revelation came, you will be attentive in your own life. We take our ordinary for granted. But it's in the ordinary where our moments pass that seem to break time to invite in grander meanings which allow us to refocus on our one true purpose.

> *"You become what you give your attention to."*
> — EPICTETUS

Sometimes honest wandering is received as prayer, as Alexander saw the High Priest of his vision in real life. And if prayer is lived and a sacrifice made, as Alexander learned, your life's purpose arrives as a revelation to see. And the best prayer of wanderers like us is always to see the most beauty arise to destroy the injustices around us.

Our prayer is to see and perhaps even participate in a maximal love because maximal love is the ultimate beauty philosophically possible. And ultimate beauty brings ultimate truth.

When I had that surgery to remove my tumor, which resulted in my brain fog, I cognitively lost a great deal. And when I slowly began to regain my mental capacity a few years later, it certainly helped. But mental strength was not the solution. I needed to evolve. I needed the humility to pray for beauty to invade the gates of my closed-off heart to right my bent mind.

Just as the Black Swan events that shape our world are enfolded in vulnerability, so too are those few personal experiences around our books and dinner tables that best make us better men.

> *"What looks beautiful, really beautiful—is also right."*
> — VINCENT VAN GOGH

A powerful revelation may strike at any moment.

But how?

* * *

The lie in the teenage love songs is the same false tale we still believe as adults. The lie is that we must search and make love work all on our own effort. The lie that we must fight and overcome our loved ones—to teach them how to be a proper man or a decent woman—and to finally defeat them with our rightness. And this hell-fashioned falsehood that our vanquished lover shall eventually love us back corrupts our souls. That is never a lovely love.

Perhaps, however, we were meant to be the ones overcome.

We want to be safe now and perhaps one day invade, when we instead need to be invaded. We want to close the gates to the risks we fear, and instead need to open up to the power which surrounds us already. To open the gates in our obedience to a stronger invading force, as the Jewish High Priest saved Jerusalem by opening his protecting gates to Alexander's army. And his opening of the protections out of obedience brought power into Jerusalem. And Alexander's power which once threatened death brought life. Life because of the High Priest's obedience and the prayer of a bloodthirsty conqueror who once bent his knee.

Perhaps, like Alexander, we are also built to find our purpose and next steps only after we cast down our crooked crowns, bow, kneel, sacrifice, and pray.

That's how I did it. Or rather, that's how it happened to me.

I WAS BLIND, BUT NOW I SEE

This was the ordinary scene Van Gogh painted: the everyday, which, when colored properly, remade the unnoticed, unknown background of proper dark contrast to transcend an ordinary family. This contrast looks like pain, friction, infertility, job problems, mental clarity, and the loss of those we still love who never loved us.

Transforming the unknown—the unnoticed ordinary—into a masterpiece is the prayer of all little girls, knowing they are meant to become mothers. Hoping that such a thing as love exists, they believe it will find them one day.

And hoping is everything.

Over the eight years of my mental fog, stemming from my tumor surgery in 2013, I silently prayed, "God give me an ounce from the ocean of your wisdom." And I prayed that nearly every day, not realizing He was trying to invade me with his gift of wisdom. But I was too guarded to let him because everywhere I looked, I saw threats instead of opportunities. I wanted the gates closed.

Masterpieces are created only after the Master is given the pieces we hide for ourselves.

It was not until February 2021, a midweek meatloaf supper with my family. Homemade mashed potatoes with the whipped buttercream and buttered sweetcorn mounded over in our matching white ceramic serving bowls. No gold. No thrones. No special guests. No wine. In our ordinary home. Around our average wooden family dinner table. A rectangular 10-seater in the breakfast nook, where the girls love to paint their yellows, blacks, and reds and leave their wash water cups for me to rinse free.

I'm never sure if I'm really sitting at the foot or the head of the table. Shannon to my left, on the chair side of the table. Lily-Kate preparing for a pending battle at lacrosse practice to my right holding down the benched side. Emerson, next to Shannon. Rosie in volleyball black pads across from me. Their iced sweet teas in tall translucent pink fractled cups. I never put enough sugar in. Swishing around searching for that perfect piece of crunchable ice. Rosie finding hers. Emerson dressed for ballet rehearsal later—not yet wearing her tip-toe reinforced pointe shoes—sliding her meat under her brown gravied potatoes with the same tarnished fake silver fork Shannon and I registered for at Dillard's nearly two decades prior. Lily-Kate asking for seconds in-between her caricatures of cartoons and our miniature goldendoodle, Bean. Shannon attempting to eat, heaping out more to keep plates full, and five napkins in five laps.

With the four girls arrayed around me, laughing, Christ blazed forth this proclamation into my heart: **I have heard your prayer for wisdom, but your gates and walls are still fearfully guarded to keep me out. So since you will not let me in, beauty's coup will unlock your gates from the inside. And I will enter. I am Wisdom.**

This single average moment raised beauty, truth, and love—all together—for my now-seeing eyes to worship the Invading Revealer as He delivered the infinite drop of wisdom to my fearful guarded depths. This sole drop brought courage to open the gates of my life to be invaded by the full force of His healing. My broken mind and bent heart straightened out that very moment from what I saw. He only uses crooked men.

My eight-year mental fog lifted at that moment. And I never told a soul until now because it was too holy to speak about with my profane lips.

I let down my guard for a single moment—a scent of the magnificent—to satisfy all the appetites of my life. Power, wealth, and fear of loss are no longer appealing to me. Because wisdom stormed over my life's fears.

Not just the girls around the wooden rectangle—which they would alone satisfy my life—but to take in a single moment into my evolving soul. At that dinner table. Mid-crunch. Mid-laugh. Their frozen movement pierced me with a moment. And its point plunged deep, as a key unlocking a medieval dungeon door. His key, beauty, pierced my cold heart as if by the fiery spear of destiny which pierced Christ's heart to ensure He was indeed dead. Both stabbings ended in more living.

I did not need to see Him on yellow thrones of gold to believe, for Christ who is Wisdom Himself was now enthroned on my weak, dead heart to pour out a living drop of Himself to meet my lone prayer.

To trust that a single glance of the ordinary is enough to make my life worthwhile and to make me into a new man. That a world-shattering moment like this happened—makes the moment I saw True. More real than real. And more real because I cannot show it to you for your scrutiny. You can never see the undestroyable. All you can see is the effects I live out in front of you.

And I'm sobbing alone in my office writing this with joy that it happened to me. I did not make it happen. I was a victim. Lanced by Wisdom Himself.

For the array of my loves, laughing and looking upon each other was indeed that perfect maximal love I had once theorized about years earlier. The shining beauty that unlocked Christ's invasion to deliver my prayers. The theory turned into fact. Prayer answered.

The maximal love there showed itself—not in a sanctuary, painting, or theater—but around a paint-stained dinner table of my daily life. The reflection of my love for Shannon, shining onto Rosie, knowing she was accepted. Rosie's acceptance budding in her anticipation of Emerson's embrace of her sistering. Lily-Kate's knowing that I would laugh before the joke's delivery, and that Emerson would see my laughter—a smile of endearment of Lily-Kate's budding personality which Emerson sisters as a master forms a clay bust over which to marvel. My laughter, evoking

Emerson's quirkily bent smile, would be seen by Shannon as a mediation of her mothering smile, and my fatherly encouragement of the silliness Rosie expected to see from her best friend, who Shannon herself bore resulting out of that collegiate love we sowed long ago.

This was the perfect scene of what every family unknowingly hoped to manifest: the bringing together of true beauty arising from the truest maximal love. This single moment of laughing during the peak of power in the bond of interlocking loves reflecting off one another.

And yes, I do mean power. The sort of power that evolves a man. He used this beautiful scene to set me right.

He slipped in a new master using beauty's coup. And an undestroyable hope. You see, everything became clearer in that moment. I now see that the first drop of wisdom with Christ's divine foot strike dropping down into Jerusalem was a mirror of what was to happen again in some of us.

He will again strike beauty and wisdom into our wandering and praying hearts if we just get our dinner tables and books in proper order.

He will again strike beauty and wisdom into our wandering and praying hearts if we just get our dinner tables and books in proper order.

And His steps will continue to invade every other part of our lives as we become shining mirrors of that first forever-strike. He showed us how to live, bow, kneel, speak, fight, and sacrifice. And it happened once for us all to see.

And if it happened once in my life—that my mortal eyes once glanced at those beauties in their innocent joy striking love at each other—a wholed family slipping the surly bonds of the whole dying world—it would give me an eternal hope that it might happen again.

And if it struck me, it could strike you.

Love can invade anywhere if it exists somewhere.

The surrounding gates and comfortable mediocrity which I thought protected me all along actually proved merely a prison to keep me from true freedom.

But I noticed it only after I prayed for wisdom.

MY REVELATION
BECAME MY EVOLUTION

I would never have known this dinner scene's true light without the darkness that preceded it. My mind had regained its imagination. And in a way, my love for them was enhanced into something greater which I saw through them.

My girls around my dinner table mirrored the sea-stormed call of Rembrandt as he mirrored the call of Christ to join a real story. The story of maximal sacrifice because the maximal love once invaded our world too. And still invades shy hearts and foggy minds like mine and yours.

That belief for some strange reason made me into a better man who would not just reject the lesser desire because he knows it is the wrong direction, but because I have found something that overbrims to flood out all my original selfish desires. Rejecting the lesser likes to embrace the higher loves. The lower facts to witness the truth.

Reject the lesser likes
to embrace the higher loves.

My desire for relevance is no longer remembered; it is no longer empowered. It has been usurped by another master—Christ. My fear and mental haze were usurped by my glance of a greater gravitational power delivered out of the beauty of my loves around that table, pulling me and bending me into its sculpted form. For as every mass bends time, so too the greater gravity always pulls the lesser.

I was being pulled forward by Christ's weight all along into stepping when I just wanted to stand there self-imprisoned in pride and safety. He, like the Sun that peeks out through the storm clouds, has a massive mass that arcs all the great literature, recounts all the years, and remakes the dinners of families.

YOUR LESSON:
A MAGICAL LIVING CANVAS

As fulfillment, not contentment, is the true inverse of desire, so too I believe that good is not the opposite of evil. Rather it is the beauty of our story brought up into this Ultimate story, that will burn up the unjust evils that pollute our blinded eyes. And that beauty of our shared story, in the midst of dark struggles, will pave the road for His wisdom and love to get into us if we will just open the doors despite our vulnerability and fear to safely do things on our own. We are like boys with tumors lying dormant for decades who must open our necks so the surgeon can dig out the enemy which has prevented us from becoming men.

He wants to overthrow the entrenched evil tyranny.

I think of Rembrandt's beautiful seascape painting which tells us the story of the stormy sea and the thirteen men being calmed. I then consider the Master Artist who conceives and executes with precision. His dark storms will come, after all. But the drop of His sunny yellow threatens your chaotic meandering.

Evil wants peace when it's in control. While beauty wishes to murder it. Beauty is a worthy but bloody conqueror.

Just like a real man.

Beauty is a worthy compass to truth.

Just like the most Masterful Artist.

Perhaps taking these 9 Steps is all you need to get there. Because sometimes steps are just strokes.

THEORY:
REMBRANDT

And here I continue speaking in the language of arbitrage and in the philosophical sense about a historical man. Do not think I am calling you to convert to a religion. I am calling you to take 9 Steps to build a meaningful life.

Remember, it was Rembrandt's seascape depiction of Jesus Christ as Master and Stiller of the storms that brought forth that speck of yellow hope in the painting. He brought peace and destroyed darkness with three mere words: *Peace, be still.* These words inverted Agamemnon's waterside prayer for peace at sea so there could still be war at Troy. Your why matters.

Rembrandt is providing us with a concentric example.

Christ is the man who walked into Jerusalem with the crowd declaring

Him king, just like Washington. Who lived a perfect life and died a perfect death all because He came, not to become king, but to evict the tyranny of taxing fear and putrid death that prevented us from knowing the pleasure of a dinner table with His Father. He wishes us to trust that His death-conquering love was the first evolution. And that His love can be mirrored into our forever life. An intrada to an eternally unstoppable hope.

He was said to have destroyed the hellish pit of death and evil, which makes Him the fountain of life and beauty if you philosophically follow it to the inverted logical end.

And that forever type of life and beauty like His can invade men like us, because it also invaded history and all decent stories. Just as Rembrandt once painted himself into his own scene of chaos and hopelessness, Christ once painted Himself into our history. Both Masters invaded the ugliness to call out to us to believe that a drop of hope exists.

And remember, Rembrandt's call out of the painting to us is an example for Christ's call to you and me in our pain: "The storms are raging, but I am Mastering them as well for anyone who wants to take the adventure with me." For Christ is also painting us into His canvas story. We must be still, as Alexander was when he prayed in solitude to hear a mere whisper. And often His whispering becomes painting.

And He will shout down the loud evils all around you with His deafening whisper.

Even the physical painting becomes an example if we will pay attention: The profundity of the story told within Rembrandt's canvas is richer only because the canvas and the paints are dead within themselves. But when active in the hands of a master, dead things have no option but to come forth in light-laden beauty. Rembrandt anoints the void of the canvas covering the frame made of an unseen tree—with his alabaster oils of paintable light invading the darkness. But it is the truly historical, time-invading Master who once hung His redeeming masterpiece on a tree as well who will paint over the voids and wrongs in your life as He did in mine. Trees frame all proper canvases, canvas the greatest books, and book-end the greatest dinner tables. A man who builds all three seriously and honestly will have more than everything.

And if you follow the 9 Steps they will brick the path there.

And you can witness this Master's work anytime, around a billion praying necks, inside a million steepled galleries greater than The Met, or in the rise of the Sun. You must look closely for the whispering lovely ordinary if you want to see real power. Real power, like truth and wisdom, arrives through beauty if you will not open the gates to Him.

A man who minds his books and dinner tables seriously and honestly will have more than everything.

If you trust His offer enough to join the adventure, then first choose a worthy enemy. Those who do always receive the power they need because they love the good and true. For Christ Himself is Wisdom and Truth. And He remakes all our voided and selfish false canvases as we look to Him like a model sitting still for a master artist. And the longer we look and read and kneel in solitude, the more beautiful He makes us.

But to live fully, you still must take up the 9 Steps in this book.

* * *

Isn't it odd for a man like me to focus his life on a single moment and draw these conclusions? Surely these are the conclusions of a madman who advocates for the brutal killing of evil. But remember loves and evils can only be rightly understood by a man who deals with them lavishly. That is my hope for you. Because it is also the pathway to creating a story people want to hear. And a life you can be proud of when His inspection surely comes. Live lavishly in the outliers of evil and love.

Live lavishly in the outliers of evil and love.

But that moment at the paint-stained dinner table also made both my obedience and transformation inevitable.

And perhaps it's possible that if one meaningful moment gives a cocky failure-of-a-man like me revelation to move up to the next level beyond manhood, so too might the most meaningful moment ever in history give you every revelation you will ever need.

Christmas could gift you an evolution.

THEORY: LOVE & VIRTUE

Your life must be taken up into service of those in your responsibility in order for you to receive the refreshing commendation of your master to whom you are responsible.

> *"Love is both the supreme strength and the utmost risk. For those whom we say we love and we do not risk, we never loved."*
> — C.S. LEWIS

This sacrifice of your wants for others' needs is the road to meaning. This is the story of all wise men.

They say Christ is the great evolutionist of your carnal body and bent mind. I believe them. They say His glimpse is the same as pure love and high truth transforming you; a higher transformation the longer you sit to be painted by the Master. And it seems true. The longer you sit, those old men will claim, the deeper the contrast between your backgrounded depths and foregrounded brights. They wrote that you feel the pains of the paints and think He is painting over when he is merely adding layers and textures. The dead men still speak truth. Because He's not interested in a two-dimensional man. He's building up a real man.

Yes, His glance threatens to transform us all. He uses tragedy, success, family, despair, embarrassment on national news, and life-changing surgeries. And depending on what sort of man you are, His piercing lance will either terrorize or transform you. Or both.

The Master Artist will not return to the yellows until He has first rinsed the dark sins and apprehensive fears from His brush.

MY FINANCIAL EVOLUTION BEGINS

And in my newly enlightened state after that 2021 family dinner, I stopped my fear. I again believed that risk was right for me. And in doing so, I stopped being afraid of risk, perceptions, or mistakes. In abandoning fear, I gained the bravery to go back into the world to reseize my relevance.

I absorbed a massive amount of information and clarity. I turned to the burgeoning commercial real estate private equity business which was basically nothing a few years prior and began with a leap.

Here's the context. In 2018, I tried to buy my dream building in downtown Houston. The three-story timbered structure with white brick facade. 110 years old and formerly a warehouse which had been converted to creative office use sometime in the early 2000s. The 103,000 square feet of flooring was century old pine. The ceilings were constructed of hundreds of massive 24-foot-long by 24-inch thick pine beams. The large handcrafted metal sliding doors throughout had been industrially welded to appear like old 1930's airplane hanger doors. And it had a retro water tower on the side lawn which it shared with a thriving college campus.

But I first found it listed for sale in 2018 only to end up in a bidding war against Uber and WeWork, from what the broker told me. Sadly, I walked away knowing I did not have the balance sheet to compete. I had economics to factor in. They merely had energy to harvest from young souls.

The owner, an eighty-year old single man, lived in the apartment in the back of the building and was always very kind to me. That sale fell through months later, but he decided to keep the building instead of relisting it. He owned it free-and-clear. I stayed in touch for nearly three years.

Every ninety days, I would check back in with him to see how his health and vacation schedule were going. I reminded him he owned my favorite building in the world and my dream was to eventually buy it from him.

And in 2021, he called me back. He was ready to sell and I was ready to buy. He wanted $10 million but I didn't have it. Knowing the real estate business, I knew I'd need a half million for working capital: a lender for $6.5 million and $4 million in cash.

I had excellent credit, so I was able to get a lender to let me personally borrow $6.5 million. But I needed $4 million more, and I only had $1 million personal cash on hand. And this is where my friends came in. Three of them invested $1 million each with me. Sight unseen.

And so I purchased, redesigned, and rebranded my favorite building, this redeveloped warehouse in downtown Houston. It sat on two city blocks of dirt, which were alone worth around $10 million without the building.

Over the next twelve months, I instructed my in-house leasing staff to renegotiate all the leases they could. It was a recklessly bold request in the most dire office leasing market in decades—we could have lost the entire tenancy and not had money to pay the mortgage payments. And taking the 90% occupied building down to 60% occupancy, the decision wiped out all $4 million of our invested equity.

The old owner wasn't willing to take on that risk, so the building was worth far less to him than it was to us. Arbitrage.

And my trust in my team proved well-founded. The building bled money for a few weeks, but we began to see the leasing pipeline fill up with new tenants wanting to move in with far higher rents than those old tenants were willing to pay. That's also arbitrage.

After less than six months, in the worst office leasing market in US history, we brought the occupancy back to 92%. Our $10.5 million investment then valued at $19.8 million. Factoring in the $6 million loan, our $4 million cash invested ballooned to over $13 million in less than a year.

We began to do it again and again.

You can arbitrage tenants and buildings like you can arbitrage watches, cars, investments, and great ideas out of art, literature, and other men's lives. Some ideas are worth far more outside their native domain.

If you visit my office today, you will see an inverted blueprint behind my desk of this building. Not just inverted, but then made bitonal to remove the waffling grays—black background with white lines. Not only is contrarian normally right. But also all decisions trend either good or bad.

Each decision leads us a step closer to heaven or hell—goal or demise—never sideways. The large corrupt tenants paying below-market rates must be evicted if you're ever to get great growing tenants paying a premium. The good masters giving good advice must be evicted from your life if you're ever to be granted a great Master who offers a real purpose.

Risk is right, when your proper sacrifice has been made and the idols of your risk-free life are destroyed.

PREPARING FOR
YOUR NEXT MOVES

I imagine one day Shannon and I taking our grandkids to meet Rembrandt at The Met. To see a great painter who is dead, but who is really still more alive than most men have ever been. Hoping he will now re-enliven our childrens' childrens' imaginations of what could be if they took on the right master and some right risk. This odd little hope is a buoy to keep us above the water through the stormy times that will surely come.

What oddity can you hope for in three months or thirty years to keep you afloat?

Don't forget that storms are always more than threats, they are also opportunities for a bath.

Those who avoid the beauty, books, boat, and the call of the master will slowly drown in their comfort and boring selfish lives. They will be said to be living while actually drowning in a lukewarm watery prison.

And yes, all who approach Christ and embrace the storms will also get wet. And perhaps plunge into the dark sea for a time. To most people these soggy souls will appear to be drowning. But they are really living free. Their oxygen is now hope.

These are the freedmen who open the gates to Christ's call now becoming the new evolution of man as C.S. Lewis spoke about a century ago.

They are merely dirty rebels bathing in the storm for a moment, only to rise clean out of the rinse water as evolved real men. With all their dimensions. Then, they will shake off the remaining chaos and leave the shade of the sunless dark comfortable clouds to bask in the Sun, who uncataracts all who look to Him for a single moment.

To try to keep your life for yourself is the surest way to lose it. For you lose everything you try to keep. But these newly evolved men who handed their lives over to Christ will rise out of certain death as sure as the Sun rose on Easter. To give your life away is the surest way to save it.

When you agree to sacrifice your life to others, and especially to God, you begin to take part in the resurrection to come. For only the dead can ever be resurrected. Only the dead want to.

Rembrandt's seascape paints that promise.

Think about the span between your now and your destiny.

- What would you do if you knew you could not fail?
- What would you do if you knew all your wrongs would be remade into rights, as layers in a masterpiece?
- What if your sinking was just to give you a quick rinse to get the mud clouding your eyes?
- What if these threats were actually opportunities?
- What if your hateful passion was hidden love?
- What would you do if you knew you could never die?

Love means accepting the unknown far too soon.

*Love means accepting
the unknown far too soon.*

Opening up the enslaving safe gates to His freeing adventure is like giving yourself fully to whatever may come.

- What would you do with the infinite courage which arrives the very moment you decide to act in giving away what you treasure most—yourself?
- What would you become if your goal was to tell a beautiful story with your life? And left the rest to chance.
- What would you become if you really believed it is only the masters who take the broken lives and build a masterpiece with them?
- What kind of good man could you become if you knelt and prayed like Alexander the Great?
- What if all along, your wandering was praying?

You'd be the sort of man others think is unstoppable. You'd always get back up after getting hit, despite wanting to lie down.

Never quit on yourself.

You'd live with abandon of what others think of you, because you'd return home to one, then two, and perhaps even three others around your dinner table who were your real cares.

You'd become the sort of real man who would not only take responsibility for his own actions, but for the finances and growth of his entire family. And perhaps for the growth and finances of an entire company or many companies who relied on you for their paychecks. And dreams.

You'd be the exhausted man who kept taking steps of faith never letting on he was tired, knowing you are sacrificing your finite todays for your infinite tomorrows because that is the wise thing to do.

You'd be the multidimensional man who is building a real life for many others to live under, instead of making excuses about why life isn't fair.

Hell, you'd even have your phone in the other room so you wake up before everyone else in the world, then grow your book knowledge and have something to give back.

You'd be a real asset to a handful of people instead of a liability to yourself.

YOUR NEXT MOVES

I suspect you have been standing around just like me. Waiting for that risk-free move to hit the jackpot of a better relationship, proximity to power, or healing.

You've been poisoning yourself with mediocre thoughts, "If I can just keep doing this work I hate for another twenty years I can get out of here with a pension. If he would just notice how smart I am, I'd earn what I want to make. If I could just stand up for myself they would stop taking advantage of me. If I could just put her in her place she'd respect me."

But now is the time for you to move.

You've already read the eight chapters on standing and what standing can become if you take a single step. But now, my friend, your standing must end:

- My standing at the cocktail tables of the GQ party in Miami surrounded by depravity.
- My standing looking at the *NBC National News* text of my embarrassment at my campaign party.
- My standing at The Met alone marveling at Rembrandt's painting of *Aristotle with a Bust of Homer*.
- My standing, as Agamemnon stood, over the sacrifice I never wanted to make and then made it for the wrong reason.
- Christ standing in that boat speaking a spot of yellow peace into the storms of our lives.
- Emerson standing en pointe all alone and vulnerable on that ballet stage.
- Washington standing up to tyranny.
- Shannon's loves standing on the line watching her run that marathon.

Your standing must become stepping to prevent your blindness from returning. When you order your steps and put a few together, perhaps you might even begin to create some traction in your life.

And, of course, traction is only friction which is turned into an opportunity to move forward. Pains, struggles, wrongs, and frictions are all just opportunities to help you move forward with more grip.

> "What looks beautiful, really beautiful—is also right."
> VINCENT VAN GOGH

And when you can put a few of these actions together with some traction and grit, you might even form a life. For a life is only a collection of actions. And actions push away the ground calling you lower to free you to chase the call, which is forward and higher.

The Sun strikes strides into momentum.

For love is always watching on the line. We deserve to see a beautiful stride, and a beautiful stride can unwork a thousand sins. Lean forward.

The central question of your life is this: Which decision gives you the most beauty in your outcome?

> *The central question of your life is this: Which decision gives you the most beauty in your outcome?*

To look clean, smart, and sophisticated? Or to be clean, humble, and simple? To take the easy path you're on now? Or to find something nearly impossible to do and cobble together the competency and courage to attack it like the great enemy of your life? Run like your loves were on the line watching you run an impossible race which the human being was never built for but knows it must complete.

I would argue the best possible story IS the best possible outcome. Your DNA software is coded in the alphabet language of stories, so you are technically built by a story.

That night at the meatloaf dinner, my family was merely reflecting the beauty of a maximal love, mirrored onto them by Christ discovered by 9 Steps. And that maximal love radiating their beauty is part of a grander beautiful story which you and I were encoded to hear.

- It's the eternal story of all children playing innocently on the summer lawn.
- The fable of dragons defeated by fearful boy-knights.
- The tales of every woman who showed a little girl how to love her own little girls one day.
- The story of giving a dead woman's husband a glimpse of his wife's memory resurrected as a precursor of what is perhaps to come.
- The story of vulnerably removing your protective guard to allow for the known world's master to meet the unknown world's Maestro— and there to bow.

Just as the third person in a family arrives through painful birth, so too does this new and richer evolution of life arrive on a rough road I did not build but know is there. This road is a story, and it leads us up out of Jerusalem to invade the rest of our low-aimed lives as it redeems our entire damned world. You must now run down that road.

> *The road is a story, and it leads us up out of*
> *Jerusalem to invade the rest of our low-aimed lives as*
> *it redeems our entire damned world.*

And running you may just mirror hope out into the despair-filled lives of those who thought the road was an aimless dirt path for old fools and never considered a promise may be possible along its route. A promise that one little girl on the lacrosse field will shout their expectation of hope into the hearts of a dozen weak-willed men who never dreamed a comeback was possible for their own little girls. And there defeat defeat.

Your hope will threaten the meaninglessness you see.

> *A drop of hope anywhere*
> *threatens defeat everywhere.*

So how do you join the type of beauty which leads you down the road toward truth? How do you embrace a story which will transform you into a real man—more real than real—because you mirror the right Master who is undestroyably present?

And once becoming that new type of forever man, you willingly and brutally savage the wrongs you see in the world, beginning with one worthy enemy. Then the next. Not because you are a brute but because you are noble.

The purpose of light is to destroy the darkness.

> *The purpose of light is to*
> *destroy the darkness.*

* * *

You are called to make a commitment and to take more than a step—perhaps even a leap. It's you who will need to decide which of these lessons and theories to keep, and which losers to toss aside.

And now would be the best time for you to grab a piece of paper and a pen. A blue Bic, like that surgeon used, if you have one. Make it a ripped-apart, used-up scrap because those turn out best. And write at the top: "my vows" and today's date.

Writing down your commitments brings them halfway home.

> *Writing down your commitments*
> *brings them halfway home.*

First, when confronted with two choices, take the difficult path which may lead to the story you'd one day want to tell your grandkids. All your decisions: wealth, strategy, career, and love, should be made on this single basis. You need a story good enough to tell if you are ever to be a real man.

Building your life on the canvas of the Master artist means becoming more than you can now fathom. For the only way he could paint us new is if he is in a higher and richer dimension than us.

He who once created all the beauty you see every morning from the voided chaos is beginning to unvoid your every mourning.

> *He who once created all the beauty you see every*
> *morning from the voided chaos is beginning to unvoid*
> *your every mourning.*

And He expects you to do something with it. So do I.

Do what Alexander the Great did. God uses liars, slanderers, and murderers like him all the time. God especially loves to invert weak men and loud women. They make for the best stories of redemption. And redemptions are lovelier than boring flat-footed leapless ballerinas. Dark paints emphasize the yellow drops of hope.

Write down one act of Alexander from the below list you know you are avoiding and promise me you will work on each day until it is done. Then move to the next.

- Pray when alone and do it for longer than you are comfortable. This is how quiet begins to evict your comfort to make a place for meaning.
- Bend your will when in the presence of a master greater than you and be quiet for longer than you think necessary.
- Ask Christ for a revelation.
- Make a sacrifice of what you value most, starting with your pride, so you can receive that revelation.
- Be lavish in your fight against your enemies who want to destroy you and those you love.
- Take smart risks. Go on the greatest adventure which will create the most legendary stories to tell.
- When in doubt, do the opposite of what the devil wants you to do.

And it's just fine, if you're like me, to have really great stories of trying and failing. If you're not failing, you're not trying. In fact, those stories are what reset your humility and provide the best wisdom. Failure, though not the optimal sage, is a worthy teacher.

Failure, though not the optimal sage, is a worthy teacher.

Second, the quality of your dinner table will determine the quality of your love. Sit down to dinner with your family, or any loving family you invite over, and observe. Observe that ordinary grandeur of the common family in their circle of sharable love. It will not look the way you expect because it is true and was not invented. They will fight and be rude. They might even burp and slurp. You want to observe people who can be honest with each other.

It's that time away from the devices and facing one another that builds a life. Because facing one another is how sharable love is reflected in us all and we begin to get a glimmer of the majestic glory of God's love.

Next on that scrap, list the two things you will commit to doing (or rules to enforce with your kids) to make sure you protect your dinner table for one hour most nights of the week. Build then defend your dinner table. Protect it like you'd protect your family. They take on the same characteristics in the end: vibrant or nonexistent.

Build then defend your dinner table.

Finally, great books of centuries past will build your future because your master makes your meaning. Your master, if weighty enough, may also break your enemy: Time. Perhaps he already has.

And of course, the only way for you to recognize the mistakes in your life is to know what is true. The only way to know if you are living a worthy story is to read the greatest books to compare notes.

A book that has stood the test of a couple thousand years can build your past into a more lovely future. And that is true. And if you let it, evolutionary.

And on that crumpled paper, list the three best possible books you suspect have most positively changed the world in order.

1. The first book, which is most important, you will read each day for fifteen minutes.
2. The second book, which is the second important, commit to reading for fifteen minutes per week.
3. And the final book should be read for fifteen minutes per month.

Start with that. But have a day and time next to each then add it to your calendar. Never watch any screens or deal with any emergencies until you have invested into Your Next Moves. Don't lay down without reading. This is your only rule for now. Use rewards if you need them and the 4-Step Action Loop.

And when you get discouraged, know there's a guy from Texas who makes more mistakes than you who prays then gets tumors healed and his broken mind restored by what he once saw in the flash of an ordinary moment. So use my story of hope to threaten all your ugly pains. I promise to pray this for everyone who reads this sentence.

If you find yourself in pain and darkness, choose the manly path of maximal beauty and purity. For beauty meets truth in the end. And that's a story hurt people need to hear from healed people like you and me. A healed man is more perfect than a perfect man who never needed to be healed. To heal a life is to love a life. And only a maximal love offers a maximal life of maximal healing.

*Only a maximal love
offers maximal life.*

Now, stop just standing, and take a step. A step, after all, is the bending of your knee to propel yourself to the next place. When you bend your knee, you use your former frictions to push off the dead place you had been standing to enter a future where life calls you to run.

And bending your knee toward the right master, as I discovered, is the only pathway to both revelation and evolution. If it happened to me it can happen to you.

Remember that a forgiven man is more perfect than a perfect man who was never forgiven.

Taking a step is making a life. Aim high, and don't be afraid to storm the dreary unknown if you suspect there's a chance a worthy master awaits. And one day you may mirror a water-walker who extracts joy from storm clouds.

Step forth as if there can be no higher act than to become a reflection of the most real love imaginable. Choose a worthy enemy. Mirror the strongest master you can find. Paint hope wherever you see hopelessness. Respect your books and dinner tables. And there you will find you've built a life of substantial meaning. More real than real.

One ounce of hope threatens to burn down a hundred nights of darkness with a single moment.

*"Wait for it patiently—
annihilation or
metamorphosis."*
MARCUS AURELIUS

EPILOGUE

> *"The reasonable man adapts himself to the world: the unreasonable one persists in trying to adapt the world to himself. Therefore all progress depends on the unreasonable man."*
>
> **GEORGE BERNARD SHAW**
> *Man and Superman*

ALEXANDER IN SAMARIA

I WANT TO SHARE with you what Alexander the Great did after he left Jerusalem. In this story, I will tie up some loose ends on the themes of the waters, great men, and a life of meaning.

It is rumored Alexander, son of Zeus, searched for something eternal to confirm his claims. The same stories emerge from the Middle East to India.

Napoleon and Hitler sought the Spear of Destiny for their world domination. But what did Alexander seek?

Herodotus, two centuries before, told of the lore of an ancient water. Alexander searched for a river that unwound the ravages of aging and injury. One that reverses death into life. Destroys destruction.

Alexander sought to see his reflection in The Fountain of Youth, just as I had seen my reflection in the maximal loves in the youthful beauties around my dinner table. It's a common meta-theme: to believe we will live because we have once seen and drunk from the ancient depths of youthful love.

Alexander the Great left Jerusalem after his dream became reality. Josephus tells us Alexander then visited Samaria, a region of half-Jews, who like us half-men invented gods to worship. They asked Alexander's permission to rebuild their temple at Mount Gerizim, which he allowed. But soon thereafter, in a moment of hate due to not receiving the same favorable tax waivers as the Jews, they murdered Andromachus, the governor Alexander placed. Alexander dismantled and destroyed first their mountain temple—then them—in BC 332. Samaria was then colonized by Macedonians. For three centuries, Samaria was irrelevantly steeped in meaninglessness. Living without purpose. Remembered only for one Great man, who once governed it from afar. Whose purpose in passing through was to search for a fountain to make the old new and the dead live. But to get it, King Alexander, that god-man, had to take lives, power, and dominance. And for three centuries nothing.

Then suddenly, Samaria's next major event inverts the last. Another

God-Man comes to Alexander's dominated to give away kingly power, wisdom, and love. The same power he received from the Ancient of Days in Daniel which the High Priest Jaddas read to Alexander in Jerusalem mere days before his traveling to Samaria. Words Alexander believed were true because they were spoken by a man who he saw in his dreams and was told to obey in his prayers as he knelt. But he was a Jew.

And the Jew arrived just as a destitute Samaritan woman came to draw water out of the desert. Out of a well. In the shadow of that same Mount Gerizim crushed by Alexander the Great. Her mediating mountain to reach heaven and find a purpose for her life was thought crushed forever. But this Jewish Rabbi, who she would later be the very first in all of history to realize was Daniel's mediating Messiah and Christ, said to her:

"Give me a drink."

"How is it that you, a Jew, ask for a drink from me, a woman of Samaria?"

"If you knew the divine gift, and who it is that is saying to you, 'Give me to drink,' you would have asked him, and he would have given you living water... Whosoever drinketh of this water shall thirst again: but whosoever drinketh of the water that I shall give him shall never thirst; but the water that I shall give him shall be in him a well of water springing up into everlasting life."

The Jew claims to create fountains of youth inside men—in their hearts. He pushes back against Alexander's irony of killing men to heal one Great man. Instead, Christ, that Jewish God-Man, will soon claim the Greatest man dying flows life like a river to heal all men.

Christ and Alexander are perhaps the only two men in history who could be called Black Swans. Both men stepped foot into evil Samaria for a Fountain of Youth: to make the dead live.

Alexander the Great's prayers materialized into Aristotle's Logos, Daniel's Messiah, and David's sea-stiller. He read of and believed in all three. And then he took a step. His decision to travel to Samaria, to find the Fountain of Youth was right. Only early. The spring water was nearly bursting forth from the dirt, but the mud would not appear for three centuries.

The Messiah, called Christ, was whom Alexander read himself in Daniel who would receive all the crowns and thrones Alexander obtained through war. Now sits at an ancient well to speak victory into Alexander's victims. The muddy dirt prophets the clear waters to come.

As Tchaikovsky's *Swan Lake* score's beauty only began to display harmonic majesty by the genius choreographers after his death, so mankind's vertical story only began to disclose melodic Truth after Alexander's death.

One day, I believe I will finally watch Emerson dance *Swan Lake* for the first time. But for now, she is still too early in her training. I know she will dance vertically as well as horizontally—not because she loves to jump but because she hates to be grounded. Life calls you to soar. To spring out of and damn that dry ground affronting you with easy pleasures. You think you want melody. But it is the harmony and contrast over the other axes that make you want to dance and spring forth life. The tune must be written first if you ever wish to dance. The painful infertility of the dirt before the rose.

Perhaps Alexander was more of a prophet than we realized: going to Samaria for a Fountain of Life. Finding not, for he was too soon. He was only writing the music for the dance to come centuries later. Perhaps me, searching for someone like Shannon in college my first couple of years there—not knowing love was still years away because we were still too young. Or Tchaikovsky orchestrating *Swan Lake* too early for its proper choreography. Emerson's training too early to dance it. But the loving, knowing, orchestrating, and training each tells you that a future fulfillment may exist.

But only if you search with all your heart as if your life depends on finding it. Because it does.

Alexander's dream of Jaddas. Jaddas' dreams to keep the gates open. Daniel's writing of Alexander. Aristotle and Plato's Logos. All linking the god-man Alexander the Great with the God-Man Jesus Christ. All coming true. In due time. In fact, the god-man Alexander steps toward Fact Himself in Samaria.

Christ, the Fact, inverts Homer's false sea waters of war and myth and truth, into genuinely peaceful waves bringing fresh life in a cup. Troughing backward to the dark of the Dao. Cresting that yellow speck of Rembrandt's sea spilling over the rim. Misting our hearts to bloom despite our deserting minds. Sprinkling our spirits with the promise that the future fulfillment of a drink may exist. The mud bubbles. Calling us forward in the midst of the gloomy shadows of our meaningless mountains. And there to live by drinking in the mythical war-turned-peace-filled waters made truer than true by the God-Man sitting at a well. A man with the crowns and thrones of a thousand Alexanders lying in his pocket. Clinking as spare change.

You must trust that a drop of divine hope will one day quench the longing for purpose in all men—small and great. And it begins with a step.

EXCLUSIVE BONUSES

For Ordering 5 or More Books

WWW.RICKWALKER.COM/BULK

ENJOYED THIS BOOK?

Tell someone by reviewing on:

Amazon.com

GoodReads

Social Media

ACKNOWLEDGMENTS

So many friends—old and new—have contributed to this project. I am certain I am missing many of them, but I'd like to give it a go regardless.

Thank you to Representative Dan Crenshaw for taking his incredibly valuable time to write the foreword to my book and for his encouragement and friendship over the years.

Thank you to Dr. Ben Carson and his team at American Cornerstone Institute for reading and blessing my original book as is.

I'd like to thank many of my friends for helping me think through this book and encouraging me not to settle. Many served as beta readers: Aaron Ammar, Scott Baker, Jarrod Bourger, Paul D. Campbell, Matt Morris, Cody Nath, Rosie Cross Prihoda, and Shannon Walker.

I appreciate a man who is perhaps one of the greatest mentors of young leaders: Kyle Vann. Kyle provided his keen insight and wisdom. Kyle has helped me through the past 15 years of struggles and triumphs in business, personal, and charitable efforts.

Ed Thomas was kind enough to meet with me very early. He gave me resources and wisdom which I never knew I needed until I was six months into this project.

For the past year, Devin Murphy has been instrumental in helping me develop my voice and personal story, then to train it into the finished product you see here. Ann Bridges provided a significant amount of insight into the editing process, publishing business, and the mentality of the target demographic from her perspective in Silicon Valley. Emerson Walker provided pinpoint editing and valuable feedback.

Thanks Mom and Dad. My Mom is the reason I have anything. She's the one who sent the first month's payment to the private college she couldn't afford in faith that I'd go and God would provide. And there I met Shannon and that gave me my girls. My Mom is the one who loaned me $1,000 to launch the first business during summer break from college. She's been the rock-solid platform for my life. I've always known she's been praying for me and believed in me.

My Dad and I are more like friends. He's the guy who rejected generations of poverty and drunkenness to give our family a fresh start. And never mentioned it. I know he doesn't think in these terms, but I'm convinced he's the one who broke a multigenerational curse on his family and is the reason our family is a family at all. I'll never forget the day we drove over the Harbor Bridge after he quit his job and left his work truck at his last company, so he could help me build the business full time. My Dad's playfulness created my greatest stories growing up.

But more than all of those, I need to thank the four girls who are the great loves of my life.

In 2008, Emerson was born. Shannon and I were thrilled. I brag that I was the first person to see her because I was watching the birth like an N.B.A. game—watching the clock on pins and needles. Emerson is our elegant eldest. She has an incredible love of learning and reading and has the grades to back it up. She's the kind of lady you can trust to do the job. Emerson is an incredible blend of artistry and competency and will surely make some man stare at her in awe of what she can do.

Then, in 2010, Lily-Kate arrived. She came fully-haired with the biggest eyes, and lit up every room. She's our passionate leader—certainly not a boring one like me. I've watched her across various sports lead teammates back from near catastrophes to victory. She doesn't accept excuses and won't back down from anyone. She's going to need that one day—to fight off temptations and hurt. She does an incredible set of animal impressions and facial gymnastics when she's goofing off at the dinner table. And if the mood strikes her right, you're in store for a hilarious time. Her sense of humor and integrity will one day force some man to seriously up his leadership game.

In 2012, Charlotte Rose gifted us with her charm. She emerged the kindest and most obedient baby we could ever know. She goes by Rosie and is our rule follower. She takes delight in watching others excel and in their happiness. She is the best servant leader I've ever seen, on the volleyball court, at the dinner table, or among her friends. She has a quiet strength about her. She loves to read books and writes the loveliest notes of encouragement. Her beauty, inside and out, coupled with her compassion for everyone, will one day make her husband wonder why such a glorious creature would ever descend to earth.

Finally, I need to thank my wife, Shannon. She is my secret weapon and best friend. Ever since she walked through those college band hall doors, I've known she's the woman of my dreams. She speaks truth into our family and has sacrificed her career and schedule for us. She's always encouraging me to be more and to do more, while holding down the fort. A spectacular Mother and a firecracker wit. I love you, Shannon Walker.

You see, in the end, I was gloriously invaded. An occupying force with fanciful nails marching to their own graceful steps. They are vulnerable and strong at the same time.

And my dream is just to be considered one of the girls.

ACTIONS FOR AN
ASYMMETRIC LIFE NOW

1. Find someone to spend your life loving. Do not love them because they are worthy, but because you are not, and need someone to love.
2. Find an evil problem to defeat.
3. Write the three hardest things you are delaying doing each Saturday morning. Do those before you can eat your next meal. Those are your only priorities. They'll get done.
4. Keep your cell phone in a different room at night. Once you're up, you're up.
5. Every person has at least 2 hours of important work to do before they look at their devices each day. And it should all be done alone in silence. Silence attracts power.
6. If you're not working 16 hours a day, five days per week, you're not even trying—yet.
7. The only people who diversify are those who think they are wrong. Go all-in—short or long—on what you know best. Look for asymmetric upside—in investments or pay-to-play opportunities. Then bet heavy and often.
8. The role of a parent is the same as the coach. You build-up those on your own team, and ruthlessly defend them against those wanting to attack them.
9. It is always worse in your imagination than in reality. Never go to bed without saying the difficult thing you are avoiding.
10. If an action doesn't have any upside, it only has risk of downside. Don't do it.

WORKS CITED

Aligheri, Dante. *The Divine Comedy.* Translation and Comment by John D. Sinclair. New York: Oxford University Press, 1939.

Bible. *The Holy Bible-ESV:* English Standard Version. Wheaton: Crossway Books, 2014.

Dostoyevsky, Fyodor. *The Brothers Karamazov.* New York: Vintage Books, 1950.

Gogh, Vincent van. *The Complete Letters of Vincent Van Gogh: With Reproductions of All the Drawings in the Correspondence.* Third edition. Boston: Little, Brown and Co., 2000.

Homer. *The Iliad of Homer.* New York: Modern Library, 1950.

Homer. *The Odyssey of Homer.* New York: G.P. Putnam's Sons, 1919.

Koch, Charles. *Good Profit.* New York: Crown Business, 2015.

Lewis, C.S.. *Mere Christianity.* New York: Macmillan Company, 1952.

Milton, John. *Paradise Lost.* Penguin Books: London, New York, 2000.

Machiavelli, Niccolò. *The Prince.* Translated by George Bull. New York: Penguin Books, 2003.

Mises, Ludwig von. *Human Action: A Treatise on Economics.* Auburn: Ludwig von Mises Institute, 1998.

Ramsey, Russ. *Rembrandt is in the Wind.* Grand Rapids: Zondervan, 2022.

Taleb, Nassim Nicholas. *The Black Swan: The Impact of the Highly Improbable.* New York: Random House, 2007.

Whiston, William. *Of The Thundering Legion.* London: Legare Street Press, 2022. Originally printed J. Senex; W. and J. Innys; J. Osborn and T. Longman, 1726.

ARTWORKS CITED

Rijn, Rembrandt Harmensz van. *Aristotle with a Bust of Homer.* Getty Images. Corbis Historical. Photographer: Fine Art.

Rijn, Rembrandt Harmensz van. *Storm on the Sea of Galilee.* Getty Images. Corbis Historical. Photographer: Barney Burstein.

Other works of art courtesy of The Metropolitan Museum of Art, New York (www.metmuseum.org) include:

- Cover and Introduction Bridge Art: *Hercules Slaying the Hydra* by Jan Muller (The Elisha Whittelsey Collection, The Elisha Whittelsey Fund, 1956)
- Step 1 Bridge Art: *Alexander Visits the Sage Plato in his Mountain Cave* by Basawa
- Step 2 Bridge Art: *Four Episodes in the Story of Hercules* by weaver Benedetto da Rovezzano
- Step 3 Bridge Art: *The Sacrifice of Iphigeniea* by Gaetano Gandolfi Rococo
- Step 4 Bridge Art: *Alexander the Great Commanding That the Work of Homer Be Placed in the Tomb of Achilles,* by engraver Marcantonio Raimondi
- Step 5 Bridge Art: *The Rehearsal of the Ballet Onstage* by Edgar Degas
- Step 6 Bridge Art: *The Golden Age* by Joachim Wtewael
- Step 7 Bridge Art: *The Lament of the Art of Painting* by engravers Cornelis Cort and Federico Zuccaro
- Step 8 Bridge Art: *Allegory of Government: Wisdom Defeating Discord* by Jacob de Wit
- Step 9 Mid Art: *Charity Seated Nursing an Infant, Another Sleeping on Her Lap and a Third Talking to Her* by Guido Reni

Additional sources, articles, and interviews may be found at **www.rickwalker.com**

BONUS VIDEO CONTENT

For more information and tools, I've put together over 150 videos, articles, and tools to help you in your journey toward a more powerful and more beautiful life at **rickwalker.com/9steps**

I conducted interviews with the following experts for you:

- **Dr. Ben Carson**, Former Secretary of Housing and Urban Development
  - Prescription for a Divided Nation
- **Dr. Louis A. Markos**, The World's Foremost Authority on C.S. Lewis, Homer, and Aristotle
  - How to Reclaim Truth and Goodness
- **Donald Trump, Jr.**
  - The Ridiculous Double Standards in Politics
- **Jonathan Pageau**
  - Symbolism, Intuition, and C.S. Lewis
- **Lee Greenwood**
  - What makes a hero?

I also recorded short lecture series and summaries such as:

- Becoming a Leader (17 video series)
- Transformational Leadership (11 video series)
- Power, Enemies, and Machiavelli (12 video series)
- Entrepreneurship, Business, & Economics (9 video series)
- World Religions (19 video series)